Spoil 'em Rotten!

Also by Ted Coiné: *Five-Star Customer Service*

Also by Jane & Ted Coiné: *Customer Delight: 135 Tips*

Spoil 'em Rotten!

* * * * *

Five-Star Customer Delight in Action

Jane and Ted Coiné

iUniverse, Inc.
New York Lincoln Shanghai

Spoil 'em Rotten!
Five-Star Customer Delight in Action

iUniverse books may be ordered through booksellers or by contacting:

iUniverse
2021 Pine Lake Road, Suite 100
Lincoln, NE 68512
www.iuniverse.com
1-800-Authors (1-800-288-4677)

ISBN-13: 978-0-595-42412-2 (pbk)
ISBN-13: 978-0-595-67995-9 (cloth)
ISBN-13: 978-0-595-86748-6 (ebk)
ISBN-10: 0-595-42412-0 (pbk)
ISBN-10: 0-595-67995-1 (cloth)
ISBN-10: 0-595-86748-0 (ebk)

Printed in the United States of America

To Joe Curtin: Five-Star friend and mentor.

* * * * *

"So," Mr. Walsh said, his tone stern as he looked at Candace across the small cafeteria table. "You want to interview me for your business class?"

"Consumer psychology," Candace said. The college senior was nervous, but tried her best not to let on.

"Why me? Why Walsh's?"

Candace cleared her throat. "Well, Mr. Walsh, you see, our professor gave us an assignment, to write a term-paper focusing on one company that out-performs its competitors in its market. It's our whole grade for the semester.

"We've been shopping at Walsh's my whole life. Your customers don't just like coming here, they *brag* about shopping here. My aunt moved out of state when she got married years ago, and she still says she misses Walsh's—she wants you to open up a store in her town, way across the country.... A grocery store!

"Yes, we get a lot of that. We've collected every fan letter from customers who've moved away and want us to move with them. We used to frame them and hang them on the wall in the associates' lounges, but now there are too many, so we rotate in a

1

fresh batch every so often. If an associate is named in the letter, he or she gets $100 cash on the spot."

"Then you see why yours is such a remarkable company, and why I'm so excited to write my report on it. I mean, a grocery store doesn't usually inspire this kind of loyalty!"

"Our customers like us. That's not so unusual, is it? I remember my Grandmother; she would only buy Tiffany stained glass lampshades. My grandparents weren't rich, and so her collection was modest, but was she ever proud to associate herself with that company.

"I travel quite a bit to various conferences, and some of my colleagues from different companies boast about the great treatment they get at some of the pricier hotels, like the Ritz or what-have-you.

"My neighbor's wife has a personal shopper at Neiman Marcus, and somehow that fact makes it into every conversation. So our customers are loyal. We're not that unique."

"But you are! Tiffany, the Ritz, Neiman Marcus… they're all incredibly upscale; what my professor calls Ultra-Retail. Many of their customers patronize them *because* they're so expensive. But Walsh's isn't like that at all! Your prices are right in line with Super Save, and Johnson's, and all the other supermarkets in the area. Price isn't what distinguishes you."

"Some people would say we're more expensive than our competition. And if you look at our produce, and our meats, and prepared foods—a lot of the stuff around the perimeter of the store—you'd be right: our prices are higher because our quality is much, much better: our customers deserve it. But in the center of the store, it's a different story entirely: our Cheerios match or beat their Cheerios every time, guaranteed. Our milk is often cheaper. We fight every inch of the way on price: our customers deserve that, too. They work hard for their money."

"So do you see why I want to write my paper on your firm?" Candace asked.

He looked at her gravely for a moment. "We're certainly no GE, Candace. Walsh's Supermarkets consists of only five stores. This despite our being in business since 1981."

"But Mr. Walsh, you're—"

"Not I. *Walsh's.* I haven't done any of this alone."

"*Walsh's,* then, is a landmark in each of the towns where you operate."

"We've got deep roots, I agree."

"Walsh's does over six hundred million dollars in business a year."

"Margins in our industry are minuscule. That number is terribly misleading."

"The company is privately owned, with zero debt."

"Don't see the point of selling or borrowing. It can only invite trouble down the road. I learned that the hard way with a previous business I owned and had to close."

"You're a generous community benefactor—"

"*I* am nothing of the sort. Walsh's is, but that's the whole company. That's 'We' again."

"Walsh's is always at or right near the top of the state's list of best employers. People love working here so much, it's hard to get *any* job at Walsh's, even as a cashier! Your turnover is unbelievably low. College kids come back to work here after graduation. A number of your former managers are now leading successful companies, and three are highly-paid consultants."

"I'm very proud of the leaders we've groomed."

Mr. Walsh looked at his watch. It seemed he was getting bored. Candace was sure he'd say no to her request for an extended interview. She had to get through to him, or there went her term paper!

"And everyone—*everyone*—always remarks upon the outstanding service they get at Walsh's."

Mr. Walsh perked up. His frown turned to a slight smirk. He shifted in his seat to an upright position.

"They tell me how great it is when they can't find something, because anyone you ask will take you right to the item, and your staff often suggests another item that will complement the one they're looking for."

"Merchandising. It's essential to the success of any retailer."

"Your lines are short. Your people are always smiling. You have so many free samples that people walk in hungry and walk out stuffed …"

"And their carts are stuffed as well. They taste our samples, prepared by our expert cooks and presented by our knowledgeable staff, and that inspires them to bring the item home to their families. Again, that's just clever merchandising."

"So is that your secret, Mr. Walsh? Merchandising?" Candace took out her small notebook and opened to page one, ready to finally dive into this interview.

Mr. Walsh stopped at her question. He looked surprised, though not actually upset.

"Merchandising? *Merchandising?!* Is that what you think has led to our continued success? We shill better than the next guy? My goodness, Candace, what are they teaching you in that school of yours?"

The blood drained from Candace's face. Mr. Walsh caught himself, waving to show he hadn't meant to hurt her feelings.

"Candace, it isn't merchandising that's brought us to where we are today. Not nearly! It's people."

"People?"

"Rather, how we handle people. We spoil 'em rotten, I'm proud to say."

"Spoil people rotten," Candace repeated. She wasn't so sure this was term-paper material. Maybe she'd have to settle for a paper on one of the Fortune 500 after all, like the rest of her classmates.

"Candace, you came to me for an interview. I'll do you one better. Keep that notebook with you at all times. You're going to be my assistant for the semester. We'll start you like everybody else, at eight dollars an hour. You give me twenty hours a week—work whenever you can, and do what I ask. You can be my eyes and ears and my right hand, all at once. And every time I think of a tip that might help you with your paper, something we do that helps us to spoil our customers rotten, I'll let you know.

"Let's aim for fifty-two tricks of our trade. I'll give you one customer service tip for every week of the year. By the time we're done, you'll have more than enough material for your paper. Sound like a deal?" Mr. Walsh rose and stuck out his hand to shake on their little arrangement.

How could she say no? Candace wondered, jumping up from the table to clasp Mr. Walsh's hand before this amazing offer disappeared from her forever. He was even going to pay her!

"I'll see you at seven tomorrow morning. Bring your notebook." Just like that, Mr. Walsh shook her hand and left—though he didn't go very far. He stopped beside another cafeteria table to greet some regular customers eating there. Candace noticed that he used their names—this despite the fact that his five stores must have thousands of similarly loyal customers.

Candace thought she had her first rule on how to spoil your customers rotten: Shake hands. Slap backs. Kiss babies. Remember names, and birthdays, and kids' hobbies. Make every customer feel as special to you as they are to themselves. **"Be the Mayor,"** she wrote at the top of her first page.

* * * * *

At six forty-five the next morning, Mr. Walsh looked at what Candace had written in her book the day before. He sighed and handed the journal back to her.

"That's good, but it's not Rule One. Are you ready for your first lesson in providing Customer Delight?" He asked with a twinkle in his eye.

"Sure am!" Candace replied. She still couldn't believe the founder of the finest customer-service company in the area had chosen her as his protégé. She opened her notebook, holding her pencil at the ready.

"The number one rule of customer service?" Mr. Walsh said. "Like people."

"Like people?"

"Like people. If you don't have a genuine interest in people, and if you don't truly just *like* 'em, you're going to have a miserable career—and when you're unhappy in what you do, you can't do it all that well."

"So what you're saying is, if you don't like people, you'll never hit that top level of customer service."

"Like people, or that Five-Star level, that top one percent, the service that shocks and Delights your customers, will never happen. Like people. It's that simple—and that hard."

Candace dutifully wrote down her first lesson:

> ### 1.   Like people

She waited expectantly for lesson number two, something much more practical, something such as, "Hold the door open for ladies and old folks." But that was it. Mr. Walsh smiled in his warm, caring manner, and walked away.

* * * * *

Candace kept busy assisting Mr. Walsh throughout the week. She observed him in action every chance she got, and began to feel she was getting the hang of some of his best tricks. She kept a mental note in the hopes of impressing him when the opportunity arose.

"Mr. Walsh," Candace said one morning. "I've been your shadow for a week now, and in all that time, I've never once heard you speak an unkind word to anyone, or lose your patience even once. You phrase your orders as requests, and you thank your associates for doing what you ask them—even though it's their job to do what you say."

"You think that as boss, I should be bossier?"

"No, sir! I don't think so at all. It's wonderful to work for someone who's so respectful of his employees! I'm just amazed, that's all."

"I'm just following the Platinum Rule."

"The Platinum Rule?"

"Sure. You know the Golden Rule."

"'Treat others as you'd like them to treat you.'"

"Exactly. Well, in management, the question isn't so much how your employees treat *you,* but how they treat *the customer.*

That's where the Platinum Rule comes in. You should write this
down:

> **2.   The Platinum Rule: treat your employees
> the way you want them to treat your cus-
> tomers.**

"I've never heard that before."

"Sadly, few managers have, either. But if you give it some
thought, it makes perfect sense. Answer me this: how many customers does a Walsh associate interact with in a single hour?
We'll go with the cashiers. How many?"

"They must see, I don't know, twenty or thirty in an hour?"

"We'll go with twenty. Multiply that by our twenty-six lines,
and again by five stores. Then multiply that by our hours of
operation, 16 hours each day. What do you have?"

"Um ..."

"A lot, that's what. Quite a few thousand—and that's just on
their way out; let's not forget about all of the interactions our
customers have at the deli, in produce, asking for something
special at the salad bar.... One customer talks to seven associates
in the twenty-three minutes she is in our store, on average.
That's a lot more interactions than any single manager could
ever hope to accomplish. So what does that mean?"

"I suppose it means that the employees have a big impact on your customers' impression of what Walsh's is all about."

"Big? Hardly! To our customers, our front-line associates *are* the company. We have food, and we have people. Great food gets them here once; great people keep them coming back for more."

"So," Candace said, the full meaning of the Platinum Rule finally sinking in, "If the associates are happy, they're going to give terrific service. The customers will be happy, and they'll come back."

"And *that's* what makes us managers happy." Mr. Walsh said.

"That's like a pair of studies I read about in class," Candace said. "Enterprise Rent-A-Car looked at its most profitable locations and realized that the sites with the happiest customers were the most profitable."

"It makes perfect sense, doesn't it? I'm amazed they had to do research to figure that out."

"Tell me about it! But there's more. PETCO analyzed their stores, and found the exact same thing. But they took it one step further: what determined which customers were happiest?"

"Happy employees," replied Mr. Walsh.

"Absolutely."

"Treat your people well, and they'll be happy. Happy associates give great customer service, and so the customers are happy. When the customers are happy, they come back and bring their friends. That makes happy stockholders."

"Mr. Walsh, it seems so basic, doesn't it? It's merely common sense."

"Indeed. But as a wise man once said, 'Common sense isn't common at all.' Or something like that, anyway." Mr. Walsh was electrified. Candace had already noticed that whenever he talked about the people working for him (working *with* him, he liked to point out; 'Walsh associates work for their families, not for me') he became even more animated than usual.

"You don't get true Customer Delight if your managers are boneheads. But we'll talk more about that later. That's enough for today."

Candace wrote in her notebook:

> 3. **Happy employees = Happy customers = Profits.**

Mr. Walsh looked at what she wrote and nodded his approval. "I couldn't have said it better myself."

* * * * *

Mr. Walsh was clearly unhappy. His brow was furrowed in that way Candace had quickly learned meant that things in Walsh's Supermarket were not to his liking.

"Candace, what's wrong with Lorna? She's forgotten the most important part of her uniform!"

Candace looked Lorna over, going through her mental checklist: Company shirt, clean, ironed, and buttoned to the top? Check. Company tie on straight? Check. Black pants, black socks, clean black shoes? Check, check, check. Her nametag: yes, there it was, right where it should be. She was perfectly attired.

"I'm not sure what you mean, Mr. Walsh," Candace replied.

"Watch closely. Something very important is missing from her uniform."

Candace and Mr. Walsh watched Lorna ringing her customers. She scanned their items, answered questions; took payment … and all in perfect attire. What on earth could she be missing?

"Candace, I'm disappointed in you. I thought you'd catch it right away. What kind of a mood is Lorna in?"

Clearly, Lorna was having a bad day. She looked like someone had run over her puppy dog. But as Candace already knew, that was just Lorna. Some days, she was great fun to be around. Some days, she was average, just like everyone else. And some days, Lorna was just plain cranky. She was moody, to be sure. Still, her uniform was perfect.

"Are you ready for your next lesson in Customer Delight?"

"Absolutely," Candace said, pulling out her notebook and pencil.

"Good. Rule number four of Customer Delight: Smile."

"Smile? That's it?"

"A smile is the most important part of your uniform." Mr. Walsh looked at her, his usual mirth completely absent from his eyes. "Seriously. That's today's lesson."

> **4.   A smile is the most important part of your uniform.**

"Abbie," Mr. Walsh said, waving over the store manager. Abbie joined them. She knew right away that something was amiss.

"What's the matter, Bob?" she asked, a concerned look on her face.

"Lorna's out of uniform," he said. "I'd like you to talk to her."

"Of course. I'm sorry you had to point it out to me."

"Not to worry. Thanks, Abbie."

"No, thank you, Bob." With that, Abbie returned to the front of the store.

"What Abbie will do," Mr. Walsh explained, "Is let Lorna finish with this customer, have someone cover her register, take her aside, and ask her if there is anything she can do to help her. Then, Abbie will let her know that a warm, sincere smile is the most important part of her uniform. If she can't smile, she can go home. But she is not to return to work if she isn't cheery. That's rule number five: Be friendly or stay home."

"But Mr. Walsh, is that fair?"

"That goes for everyone else, too, including us managers. So yes, it's completely fair."

With that, Mr. Walsh flashed Candace his million-dollar smile, and left to go talk to a customer. Candace wrote her next rule:

> **5.   Be friendly or stay home.**

* * * * *

The next day, Candace reported to work after she got out of class; the noontime rush was just coming to an end. When she found Mr. Walsh, he was busy bagging groceries at one of the checkout lines, exactly as she'd seen him do a hundred times as she was growing up. He looked rather out of place laboring like that in his suit and tie.

"Ready for work, sir," Candace said in her typically upbeat way.

Mr. Walsh nodded at her to indicate he knew she was there, finished bagging the order he was on, thanked the gentleman whose order it was, and then called to a bagger to take over for him.

"Morning, Candace," he said. "Rule number six: get your hands dirty.

"Stop me if I've already told you this one—it's one of my favorites. Back when we still only had one store, I was at this big industry convention, and I was part of a round-table panel: sure, Walsh's was small, but we were already well established by that point. Anyway, most of the participants were great, but this one guy, some executive with a flashy title from a big chain across the country, didn't like what I had to say about "the brass" pitching in to help when it got busy. I'll never forget what he said, or the sneer he wore when he said it, either." Mr. Walsh screwed his face up into a scowl, and took on a disdainful tone. "'If you did better planning in your offices, you wouldn't have to work in the store during peak hours.'"

"Man, did that burn me up. And for a couple of years, I had to deal with this humiliating jerk every time our organization met. Finally, maybe three years later, he wasn't there at our annual meeting. Turns out, the guy got fired—and none of his peers would hire him, that's for sure! So my guess is that he's out of the grocery business altogether."

"You can't argue with success," she said. She opened her notebook and wrote,

6. Get your hands dirty.

Candace thought for a moment. Something didn't sit right. "Okay, Mr. Walsh: I can see how this is a great leadership lesson, but customer service? How does this pertain, exactly?"

"Getting a few managers on the floor helping to bag groceries or slice cold cuts or run to the back to restock shelves may make a small dent in the total work that needs to be done during an unexpected rush, but there's a good chance it's not going to completely solve what is clearly an under-staffing issue.

"However, think of the *perception* of the customer. It's busier than you're used to, and there's a longer wait at the deli, in the bakery, and the checkout: whatever. Maybe you're hungry, which is what brought you here at this time in the first place—that's been known to happen, hasn't it?"

"You can say that again!" Candace and Mr. Walsh shared a good laugh.

"All of this waiting is bound to make you cranky—and you're going to want to take it out on the staff, especially on the managers, who you're sure are goofing off in an office somewhere while you suffer. But wait! There's the store manager there, the top dog, and he's got his suit jacket off. His sleeves are rolled up. And he's stuffing groceries in a bag as fast (yet carefully) as he can. 'Oh,' you think. 'I guess the management here *does* give a darn. My boss would never do this kind of grunt work. It seems we customers are important to this company's leadership after all!'

"See, Candace?" Mr. Walsh continued, "Customer Delight isn't about getting it perfect every time—although we definitely try. More than perfection, it's about putting on a great show, proving you care, and making sure your customers know how much you value their loyalty."

* * * * *

"Mr. Walsh," Candace said, "I've given a lot of thought to the Platinum Rule. You say treat your employees the way you want them to treat your customer, but that's a rule for managers. What do you tell your front-line workers to do?"

"Have you ever heard of Stew Leonard's? It's the World's Largest Dairy Store—which might not necessarily be saying much, except that they sell an awful lot more than milk and eggs by now. Their stores are huge, and, although there are only a few of them, they sure are profitable. They're *always* busy, even off-hours. You should see the volume they do!"

"Sounds like Walsh's," Candace ribbed him.

"That's no mistake. We've learned a lot from other companies, including Stew Leonard's. What I like best about that outfit is what's written in stone outside of their front entrance. It's chiseled into an actual piece of, I don't know, granite I guess, and every customer and employee has to pass this eight-foot-tall monument to customer service every time they enter or leave the store. There, inscribed in stone, it says—" Mr. Walsh took Candace's notebook and her pen, and wrote,

19

> **7.   Written in stone at Stew Leonard's:**
> **Rule #1 ~ The customer is always right.**
> **Rule #2 ~ If the customer is ever wrong,**
> **reread rule #1!**

"Are customers ever wrong?" Mr. Walsh asked. "They're people, right? Of course they're wrong. But who cares!?! That doesn't matter one bit. What matters is, are they happy—are they Delighted, in fact? I'd rather lose an argument than lose a customer."

"Oh, I like that one!" Candace said. "Can I add it to the list?" Mr. Walsh nodded his assent.

> **7.5 It's better to lose an argument than a**
> **customer.!**

"Now, tell me," Mr. Walsh said. "How does that rule play out in real life?"

"Well," Candace said enthusiastically. "If your favorite color is yellow, how am I ever going to convince you that your favorite color is really blue? I might talk more forcefully than you, and get you to shut up, but that doesn't mean your preference really changed; just that I'm a blowhard and you're going to buy from someone who allows you to like yellow without a hassle."

"Yes …?"

"So in the grocery business, if someone comes in dying for Velveeta, and you tell them that's no good, they should try this Havarti with dill instead, and you refuse to even *carry* Velveeta…. There goes another customer to Franklin's Grocery Mart down the street.

"Bottom line?" Candace concluded, "Suggest the Havarti, but don't be pushy about it, and make the Velveeta available."

"I think you've got it. Now, what about a complaint about a rude associate—say, one you *know* would never be rude. So you're quite sure the customer is mistaken."

Candace thought a moment before replying.

"Well," she said, "if a customer feels that someone's been surly with her, then the fact is, that's how she feels. You can't change her perception, just as you can't change her favorite color or cheese preference. If you contradict her and tell her what a great guy the associate is, that's telling her she's wrong—she's either stupid or unreasonable. That violates rule 7.5—you'll win the argument, but lose the customer."

"Okay. So you should agree with her that the associate was wrong, even though you know that not to be the case?"

"Well…." Candace didn't like where that path was leading her.

"If you don't support your associate in this instance," Mr. Walsh said, "then aren't you violating rules two and three? You're betraying your associate, aren't you? And remember, this is an associate who is an asset to your company. Won't this wreck his morale, and quite possibly the morale of his coworkers as well?"

Mr. Walsh's eyes sparkled. He knew this was a tough one, and he clearly enjoyed watching his student struggle as she worked out the right thing to do. Candace understood that by making her think like this, he was forcing her to grow. Difficult as it was, she appreciated the challenge.

She tried again. "Seems we have a problem here. Are you loyal to your associate, or to your customer?"

"This is as real as it gets," Mr. Walsh said.

"I may have a compromise," Candace said. "You apologize for how she *feels*. You're sorry she feels that way. You'd like to assure her that, as your customer, her happiness is paramount."

"… And what if she still insists you punish the associate?"

Wow, Candace thought. *He sure isn't letting me off easy!* To Mr. Walsh, she said, "How 'bout we take it from the top: tell her you're sorry she feels insulted. Her happiness is important to you. What can you do to make her feel better? Get her thinking about compensation. Try to distract her from her desire for retribution."

"How can you make her feel better?" Mr. Walsh asked. "She says, 'I'll tell you how. That discourteous clerk needs to be fired! At the very least, reprimanded!' Now what do you do?"

Candace shook her head. "This is a tough one," she said. "What *do* you do? You've got two sets of rules in complete contradiction of each other."

Mr. Walsh saw that he had stumped Candace. He relented; after all, she was a college kid. She had never managed a single person before.

"This is one of the toughest dilemmas in management, Candace. Life is messy, and situations like this are bound to happen. You must be flexible. My first response to you is, you have to feel your way through this one. Exactly what happened? That matters a whole bunch.

"But I can't let myself off the hook that easily. Here's what I'd do: in a situation where you have an irate customer who insists you take action, a regular whose business you cherish, and an associate who is a real keeper, you've got a true conflict. You're going to have to stick by your associate."

"Really?" Candace said. "Interesting."

"Say you're sorry she feels that way—you were right-on there. Assure her you'll do anything you can to make her happy. But if she insists on punishment, be firm—gentle, but firm. This is when, after trying to avoid it as much as possible, you're going to have to make a stand. Let her know that this associate is one of your best; that you're proud of him, and you're surprised he would ever intentionally insult any customer of yours. Tell her you'll talk to him about it. That may make her back off—'I'll talk to him about this.' You're not promising any sort of chastisement at all. If that phrase doesn't satisfy her, give her another 'I'm sorry.' Keep it at that. Stick to your guns. Now it's her turn to react. If she leaves over this incident, that's unfortunate—but if this guy is as good as all that, your business needs him more than one customer, even a regular."

"Won't she tell her friends? Won't the company suffer?"

"Life is messy," he repeated. "This situation doesn't happen often—usually, either you know she's a crack-pot who will *never* be satisfied no matter *where* she shops, or he's a less-than-perfect employee, and it's quite possible he really did alienate a shopper.

"If she tells all her friends? You know, I've talked to some of those friends, ones that have been told how we mistreat our customers." Mr. Walsh whispered conspiratorially, "Wanna hear something great?"

"Sure!" Candace replied.

"Those friends tell me about it *while they're shopping here.* They know their pal's story doesn't ring true! They know that because we're Walsh's. We just don't treat our customers that way."

Mr. Walsh couldn't have been happier with himself. It was patently obvious to Candace that the pride he took in his company was at least as important to him as anything else in his life. Walsh's Supermarket Company was an extension of who he was as a person.

"Here's rule number eight. Write this down:

> **8.   Earn your chits.**

"Jack Welch said the same thing in his book, *Winning,*" Candace said.

"That's where I got it. I love that book. Earn your chits: do it right all along. Then, when you drop the ball—which we all do, no matter how good we are most of the time—people will give you a break. That one lesson alone is the foundation for any successful business."

On Saturday, Mr. Walsh met Candace at the store near her college, where they usually met. They were not scheduled to open the doors for another half hour, but Mr. Walsh was already looking frazzled. As soon as he saw Candace he held out a set of car keys.

"It's time to earn our pay, Pal," he said. "There's a bridge out between here and the city, and our milk truck is stuck in traffic. There's no saying when they're going to get a lane open for them. I need you to fill this station wagon with as much milk as will fit, and drive out to the other two stores to our south."

Candace nodded dutifully.

"And it gets better. At your first stop, drop off half the milk and fill back up with bread—the manager there knows which kind. We goofed up on the order. The bread *and* the remaining milk goes to your second stop. There, unload everything, and then you're a chauffeur: we're short-handed here, and they're going to loan us five associates.

"Don't speed, but don't waste time. We can't let our customers down! They're counting on us to have this stuff for them."

Candace nodded again, committing it all to memory: she never wanted to let Mr. Walsh down. His respect meant that much to her.

Just as she was about to leave, he said, "Candace, what's the lesson here?"

"That's easy," she replied with a smile of her own. "The show must go on!"

"I knew you were a quick study," he said. "That's exactly right. Number—what is it, eight?"

"Nine."

"Rule number nine: the show must go on. If you're out of milk, get some milk, because your customers are going to be looking for it, and their kids won't be let down."

"That's right," said Candace. "If we don't have milk for them, our customers will go across town to Super Save to get it."

"… And no sane businessman wants his customers setting foot in his competitors' store, even just one time."

Candace pulled out her ever-present notebook and wrote,

> **9.   The show must go on.**

She thought a moment. "You know," she said. "This reminds me an awful lot of Disney. Everything there is compared to acting: employees are called cast members, work is put in terms of a performance …"

"I love Disney parks," Mr. Walsh said. "That company's a little like a cult, but it's a cult of Customer Delight. That's the kind of cult I wish more people would join."

* * * * *

"Mr. Walsh, I was thinking about yesterday's lesson, with the milk and bread," Candace said.

"Oh, that's right! You did a great job, by the way. Thank you!"

"Thank you?" Candace laughed, incredulous. "I was just doing my job. It's not like I could have said no."

"But you still helped us out, and I'm grateful. Thank you."

"I guess that's the Platinum Rule again, Mr. Walsh: you're always thanking your associates and managers for doing what you tell them to do."

"I try not to *tell* anyone to do anything," he said.

"Good point. You ask. But Platinum Rule or not, that's kind of funny, your being the owner and all, isn't it?"

"I suppose," he said patiently. Candace could feel that he sincerely liked her. It meant a lot to her.

"But here's a question for you, Candace: do you like it when I ask you to do something?"

"Well, yes, as a matter of fact. I like it a lot."

"And when I thank you for doing what, as you point out, is merely your job?"

"I think everybody appreciates that about you. I certainly do."

"There's two more rules for you: Ask, don't tell. And be generous with the Thank you's. After all, they're free."

Candace wrote,

> **10. Ask, don't tell.**

> **11. Thank your associates—often and sincerely.**

"Good. I'd say you've got it. A boss who bosses his people around is ineffective. Nobody's going to forget who signs the paycheck and makes the schedule. They'll do what you ask of them. So why not be pleasant about it?

"Now what was your question for me?" Mr. Walsh asked.

"Oh, it wasn't a question: I just wanted to share some wisdom passed down from my swim coach when I was little. We'd just lost a swim meet, and a lot of us kids had done pretty badly on the individual level. Everybody was complaining about how our coach was working us too hard in practice, and we had too much homework to sleep enough, and the meet was so far away that the car trip had sapped us of our energy—you get the idea.

"And your coach said, 'Excuses are like feet. Everybody has a couple, and they all stink.'"

Candace's jaw dropped open. "How did you know?"

"Your coach was Chuck Krein, right?"

"Yes, that's right."

"Chuck used to be on night crew at our first store. He got that from his night manager, Mike Warner."

"I don't believe it!"

"Small world. It's a perfect tie-in to "The show must go on." Your customers don't care one bit why you haven't got their milk. Much as they love you personally, or even love your store, they've still gotta feed their family. So when you tell them why you can't come through for them, you're wasting your breath. Come through for them."

12. Excuses are like feet: everybody has a couple, and they all stink.

"Alright, Candace; quick quiz: What's the magic word in Customer Delight?"

There was mischief dancing in the corners of Mr. Walsh's eyes as Candace pondered his question. Clearly, he was waiting to share one of his favorites with her. Also clearly, the magic word he referred to couldn't possibly be *the* magic word everybody learned as a kindergartener, 'please,' because that was too obvious. Candace wanted to get this one right so she could impress her mentor.

"I'll give you a hint," he said in his playfully impatient way. "It's also the magic word of teaching, and coaching, and parenting, and managing.... Any idea now?"

"It isn't, 'thank you,' is it?" she asked uncertainly.

"Thank you? No." Mr. Walsh positively glowed, he was so proud to be stumping her. "Not even close."

"Do I get a second chance?"

"Why? Why do you think I should give you another try?"

"Because—"

"That's it! You guessed the magic word on your second try!"

"I didn't guess anything yet," Candace said, bewildered.

"'Because' is the magic word. In customer service, as well as in managing, and parenting, and many other endeavors, 'Because' is the magic word."

"Huh?"

"That word alone has a magical quality that puts people at ease. Better write that down now."

---

13. *"Because"* is the magic word.

Mr. Walsh continued. "We all have an inner drive to find meaning in anything we do or experience. If you say 'No' to a customer, what have you done? You've alienated her. If you say, 'Sorry, we can't,' or, 'It's against policy,' or 'One hour from now is too soon,' then you're antagonizing the poor customer. What you say is 'We can't,' but what she hears is, 'We don't *want* to because we don't care about your needs, or about your patronage.' When we don't give people reasons, we don't give them our respect."

"But Mr. Walsh," Candace stammered.

"Yes?"

"In our last talk, you told me that customers won't accept excuses. You told me to give them what they ask for, or you're sunk! Now you're saying the exact opposite: 'This is how you make excuses.'"

Mr. Walsh shook his head. "Not at all, not at all. An excuse isn't a reason; it's a way of letting yourself off the hook. A reason is what you always—always, always, *always!*—provide when there's simply no way you can comply with a request. Let the customer know why. Let them see things the way you do, so they buy into what you're telling them. That way, you're not letting them down, you're *explaining*."

"I see," said Candace, although she didn't really see yet.

"'Because' is the magic word," Mr. Walsh went on. "Say a man calls up and needs a full-sized sheet cake for his daughter's birthday, and he needs it in an hour. He wants chocolate and vanilla marbled, with white frosting and pink and yellow flowers. You don't have any full-sized sheets of any flavor, and it takes at least two hours to mix, bake, cool, and decorate from scratch, even if you're able to drop every other order just to satisfy him. What do you do?"

"Well, I've never worked in the bakery, so this is a tough one. At Walsh's, I've already learned that 'No' is a four-letter word...."

"You should stop right now and jot that down. It's one of my favorites."

Candace did as she was told:

> **14. *"No"* is a four-letter word.**

"It's not 'No,' then," Candace thought aloud. "And we wouldn't say, 'There are people here who I have to help before I can get to you....'"

"If one of our associates ever said something like that ... Oh, boy."

"No, absolutely never. But one hour, huh? Gee, that's a tough one." Candace thought for a moment more; then, suddenly, she brightened. "I know!" she exclaimed. "I'd explain the lack of full-sized marbled sheet cakes—'I'm sorry, sir, but we don't have any here at present, and it takes at least two hours to mix, bake, cool, and decorate one (you can't decorate a hot cake). But, we do have half-sheets of marble cake. Would you like me to put two together? We'll spread the icing so she'll never notice the split down the middle."

"I like it. You're a problem solver." Mr. Walsh nodded. "Or ...? What else could you say?"

"Or ... we could do half a sheet of chocolate, half of vanilla, to make it look like you ordered half & half on purpose."

"Good, good. Or ...?"

"Or, we could call another of our stores and, if they have the sheet ready, they could drive it over here really fast."

"That's another option. Or ...?"

"Or ... Let's see, or we could drive it out to his house when we're done, for our usual small delivery fee. Would he like some ice cream with that? Ben & Jerry's, perhaps? And does he have paper plates and cups to match the yellow and pink flowers on the cake? How about a mylar balloon? We could deliver the whole shebang."

Mr. Walsh held up his hands in mock surrender, laughing hysterically. "Okay, okay, Candace, I'm convinced: you're a merchandising guru! That's brilliant. But let's backtrack a bit, and review how this potential disappointment—hey, it's his daughter's birthday and he almost forgot, so let's call a spade a spade: this potential *catastrophe*—can turn around, with the right finesse.

"First of all, nothing you do or say is going to get that cake made in time—and that call to the other stores is inspired, but what if they're out, too? So you may have to let him down on his initial request. But don't leave it at no! Say 'We can't, *because* ...' and then fill in the reason. Then, give an attractive alternative! Problem-solve! Snatch Delight from the clutches of disappointment! Did I say that?" Mr. Walsh asked, obviously tickled with himself. "You can quote me. In fact, all kidding aside, better write this down."

15. Instead of "No," Make it happen!

"That's getting the cake from another store," Mr. Walsh said. "It's tough, but it's worth it to see the look of gratitude on that daddy's face when you come through—and I've been that dad, and that husband, enough times to know exactly how he feels. So the most important thing is to make it happen.

"But sometimes you can't make it happen—as when you have to cook the cake from scratch, and one hour simply won't do it. Or when you have to combine two smaller cakes for the guy. So here's how that goes:

> **16. When you can't say Yes:**
>   **1)   Say you're sorry—and mean it.**
>   **2)   Explain why not (use the magic word).**
>   **3)   Suggest an attractive alternative.**

"There are all sorts of situations where you just can't say 'Yes,' and that's that! A customer wants to reach into the lobster tank and grab his own lobster. What happens if our associate says yes, Candace?"

"The Health Department shuts us down!"

"Sure, so 'No' isn't negotiable in this instance—at all! But that's okay. The associate says 'I'm sorry, but that's not possible, *because* the health department prohibits it.' The guy may not like the answer, but he's got a reason, so it isn't just some frivolous rule made by nameless, faceless Walsh's upper management—it's a state law, and Walsh's can get in huge trouble. So he's already thinking, 'I don't like it, but I'd better give this guy a break, because it's not his fault.'"

"Then," Candace jumped in, "the fish associate says he'll be happy to pull a few out and let the man choose, as long as he knows he can't touch. And voila! Everybody's happy."

"Everybody," Mr. Walsh agreed. "It's the power of the magic word: Because."

* * * * *

Candace took her change and picked up her bag of groceries. "Thanks, Peggy," she said.

"No, thank *you*, kiddo," Peggy said, a warm smile across her face. Candace loved the instant familiarity she'd gotten from Peggy. Somehow, the cashier pulled that off with everyone in the store, including Mr. Walsh (whom she called Bobby) and any number of customers, even the snooty types. Peggy was the real thing, and everyone loved her for it.

Candace was about to walk away when she stopped dead in her tracks. A light bulb went off in her head. She looked behind her, and there was no one waiting, so she decided to pick Peggy's brain a bit.

"You know what I haven't heard once in a Walsh's, ever?" she asked. "'No problem.'"

"And you never will. *Of course* it's no problem for us to help our customers, Candace! It's our job!"

"That's a good point. It's pretty weak to say 'No problem,' come to think of it. Not exactly Five-Star."

"For that matter, 'You're welcome' doesn't inspire any Customer Delight either, does it?" From the expression on her face, Candace could see that Peggy was proud of her expertise in the area of Delighting the customer.

"Now what's wrong with 'You're welcome?'" Candace asked.

"It's polite."

"Sure it is. But it's only three-star."

"I'm not as familiar with the star-rating as I should be," Candace said. "I know hotels and restaurants use them, and the more stars the better, but after that, I'm in the dark." She thought a moment. "Oh, and AAA uses diamonds, but I think they're the same as stars."

Peggy cocked his eyebrow. "Of course you don't know this stuff," she said, chiding herself. "Why would you? Okay, here's a quick run-down of the five stars. You can write it in your book. Although it isn't a "rule," it is great to use the stars as points of reference."

Candice wrote what Peggy told her:

Zero-Star:	**Enraging (bottom 1%)**
One-Star:	**Horrible (2–11%)**
Two-Star:	**Disappointing**
Three-Star:	**Unnoticeable**
Four-Star:	**Excellent (89–99%)**
Five-Star:	**Stupendous! (Top 1%)**

"You can save the in-depth analysis for another day," Peggy said. "The bottom line is that most businesses provide two-and three-star service, and that's why they have to struggle so much. Here at Walsh's, we aim for Five Stars in everything we do, all day long. We are terribly embarrassed when we slip down to Four Stars."

"Embarrassed by 'Excellent' service!" Candace said in awe. "Before I started this project, I never would have believed that possible. Now, though, I understand it's true."

"Anyone can be excellent if they make an all-out effort, Candace," Peggy said. "But why settle for second best, when you've got the best people on board? Why not go for it?"

Peggy collected her thoughts. "I think we were discussing three-star service, weren't we? Here's why it's so bad: your customers don't even notice it. It's like 'Have a nice day;' it means nothing any more. You see, Candace, every interaction we have here at Walsh's can go one of three ways: it can insult our customers and drive them away, like 'No problem.' It can make no impression at all, and inspire no loyalty, like 'You're welcome.' Or, it can make a lasting impression and make our customers love coming here. For that, Mr. Walsh encourages us to say things like, 'My pleasure' and 'No, thank *you.*'"

"'My pleasure;' there's another one I hear all the time around here. 'I'm happy to help' and 'I'm Delighted to be of service' are good ones, too. I think you're right. When I say 'Thank you' and you answer with 'My pleasure,' I think to myself, 'Boy, what a special place. These people are actually pleased to help me! I'm coming back!'"

"That's the idea, Candace. We want them to keep on coming back. Profits mean job security for all of us."

"Okay, Peggy. Thanks for the lesson. Have a good weekend."

"You have an awesome weekend yourself, kiddo!" Peggy replied.

Outside of the store, Candace opened her notebook to a new page and wrote,

> **17. Every interaction can go one of three ways:**
> 1) **Insulting**
> 2) **Neutral**
> 3) **Delightful**

> **18. Replies to 'Thank you:'**
> * **No Problem.**
> *** **You're welcome.**
> ***** **My pleasure.**

With Rule #5 in mind, Candace wrote,

> **19. Profits = Job security.**

* * * * *

Candace knew that she was on to something big after her talk with Peggy. While Mr. Walsh's insights were priceless—how many college kids get anywhere near a completely self-made tycoon, except maybe to carry his luggage?—the things she could learn from his staff would be important, too. Besides, she suspected he might be impressed with her if she did a little research on her own, and this was a perfect time to do it: he was away on a business trip for several days.

So she set out to talk with some of the front-line staff at Walsh's. Her first chat was with one of her favorite associates, Juan, of the dairy department.

"Juan, do you mind if I ask you something about your work here?"

Juan handed Candace two crates full of half-n-half. "I'm happy to oblige. Let's talk as we walk, amiga."

Candace accepted the crates and fell into step with her friend.

"What one thing can you tell me about the way things are done here that makes for such a customer-centric company culture?"

"Customer-centric, huh?" said Juan in his lightly-accented English. "I like how you put that. Now, what do we do that

42

encourages our focus on the customer? That's easy: we all speak English."

"Huh?" asked Candace. "Of course you do—"

"Of course? Hardly! When I first got to this country, I didn't speak a word of English. If someone said 'Hello,' I'd say 'Thank you.' If they asked me my name, I'd say 'Me Guatemala.'"

"But that must have been a long time ago," Candace said. "You must have come here as a little kid. Your English is great now."

Juan shook his head. "I came here six years ago. The first six months, I was cutting sugar cane in rural Florida for twenty bucks a day. When the foreman decided he'd pay us, that is."

"No!"

"Oh, yes. Not every employer is like Mr. Walsh. We were illegal; he'd remind us ten times a day that if we fell out of line, he'd turn us over to INS. We didn't complain."

"But … Twenty dollars a day?" Candace asked, eyes wide in disbelief. "Why work at all?"

"Gringa," Juan said affectionately, "Twenty dollars a day is a fortune in my country. Even after paying for food and use of a bed for eight hours, I was still able to send money home to my family."

"I never knew …"

Juan kept on with his story. He wasn't looking for sympathy. "Fortunately, my sister Rosa got in touch with me; told me she had a great job with a wonderful company here, at Walsh's. She sent me a bus ticket, and I came right away. Because she's a citizen and close family, I was able to get a *carte verde*—a green card. Walsh's hired me my first day in town."

"But you said you didn't speak any English at all. Did you pick it up in Florida?"

"On the plantation? From who? The only guys there who weren't from Guatemala were from El Salvador. The guys who weren't from Salvador were Mexican. Even the foreman, the guy who stole from us, was Mexican." Juan sighed, thinking of his time cutting sugar cane. Then his expression lightened up considerably.

"So my point isn't how tough life can be for illegal immigrants. My point is, I showed up here for work, and I couldn't understand anybody. The manager gave me a mop, and Rosa or another Hispanic associate would have to translate for me, tell me where to clean. I'd try not to look customers in the eye, because I couldn't answer their questions. You can't Delight your customers when you have no idea how to communicate with them."

"That must have been tough," Candace said.

"I think it was worse for the customers and the managers than it was for me. I remember this one time, Donny, a manager at the time, had this Clifford costume he'd rented for the day for some kids' promotion—you know, The Big Red Dog. When the event was over, he gave the Clifford suit to me and asked me to put it in his car so he could return it. I misunderstood and threw it in the dumpster." Juan rolled his eyes. "You should have seen how angry he was when he finally found out. There were fish guts and all sorts of stuff all over it. 'That's gonna cost us $300, Juan! You're killin' me!' he said. I thought for sure that I'd be fired, maybe even arrested—how did I know how the law works here? But instead he caught himself, and just started shaking—not with anger, but laughter."

"So how did you learn English?" Candace asked.

"I don't know if there was any connection, but about a month later, a dozen of us immigrants are called into the conference room. Bob Walsh and Donny are there with some guy in a suit, like them. Bob introduces this guy as an English teacher. The teacher, El Diablo, explained that we needed English if we were ever going to get moved to full-time, or get a promotion. 'Who wants to become store manager?' he asked. 'They make a lot more than a bagger or maintenance guy, don't you, Donny?' Bob and Donny nodded yes. 'A lot more!' Bob said."

"Juan, wait a minute. Doesn't 'El Diablo' mean The Devil?"

Juan laughed. "Absolutely!" he said. "That teacher worked us like you can't imagine! He was full of energy, funny as heck, but he never let up. Twice a week, for two hours each time, for nine months straight, we worked, and practiced, and learned … it was tough! But before the end, I was talking on the phone with customers, taking orders for birthday cakes, you name it."

"That's amazing progress!" Candace said. "I'm taking Spanish in college now, and I took it in high school, too. I don't think I can go two sentences without breaking into English, and that's after five years of classes!"

"You need El Diablo," Juan said. "His company's motto reads: 'Fun and exciting; fast and effective.' Every word is true."

"To get back to my original question," Candace said, "you think Mr. Walsh's commitment to your learning English is a customer-service issue?"

"Is it ever!" Juan said. "First off, it shows us he cares about us. Other companies don't teach their employees English, and those employees don't hesitate to switch jobs at the first chance. I'm never leaving—all twelve of the students in our class are still with the company, five years later. And because we're so loyal to Walsh's, we treat our customers great—because we know how important that is to Mr. Walsh, our patron.

"Secondly, we can talk to the customers now. So nobody's getting frustrated because of the language barrier.

"The thing is, Candace, there is no company in the state that doesn't need immigrant labor. There just aren't enough Americans to fill all the jobs, especially the entry-level stuff. That's where we come in: we're hungry for opportunity, and we're not really motivated to take vacations, or take Sundays off, either—we've got the American Dream to pursue! So a lot of employers say we make great workers ... but then they complain that, if only we spoke English, we'd be perfect for them. Well, Bob Walsh taught us English. We're ten times more valuable as workers than we were before. He doesn't complain the way those other bosses do."

"That's Mr. Walsh for you," Candace said. "He doesn't make excuses; he gets results."

"He's a smart man," Juan agreed. Then he asked, "Out of that class of twelve students, guess how many are full-timers now?"

"Um ..."

"Ten. Five of us are department managers or assistant managers. One of the original twelve made it to assistant store manager—in just five years, from bagger. No one's ever risen that fast before. He'll be general manager one day, too. You wait."

"And you all give service with a smile."

"We have a lot to smile about," Juan said.

Candace realized they had stocked all of the creamer while talking. She was holding two empty cases.

Juan held out his hand. "I'll take those, Candida," he said. "You've got some writing to do in your little notebook, I think."

And she did. Candace wrote,

> **20. English only at work. (So teach your staff. It's worth the investment!)**

* * * * *

The next associate Candace talked to was Roberta, a quiet woman who divided her time between cashiering and the salad bar. Candace's assignment that afternoon was to 'shadow' and assist Roberta as she restocked and tended the salad bar, and so over the course of a few hours she'd gotten Roberta to open up a little.

"Roberta," Candace said as they sat down for a coffee break. "What does Walsh's do right that other companies don't?"

Roberta's eyes lit up in a way that Candace hadn't seen before. It was plain to see that Candace had hit on a favorite topic of hers.

"For one, no waiting. If there are two customers in a line to check out and a third approaches, we quickly open another line, even if it's just for that customer. Here's something for your notebook:"

> **21. Two to a line, <u>Max!</u>**

"That's a big one around here. Mr. Walsh doesn't even like to see a *single* customer waiting, not to mention two!

Candace wrote,

22. "Our customers don't wait."

"The same thing goes for the deli. My boyfriend Tony is assistant deli department manager. He says that's where all the angry customers go, to take it out on you, for some reason—who knows?" She reflected on that for a moment.

"But I *do* know, at least for part of it: in the rest of the store, you shop at your own pace, get what you want, and nobody holds you up. But ever been to another supermarket? Super Save is the worst at this: they'll have a line around the block waiting for cold cuts, and only three clerks on duty. Mr. Walsh says that's one of his favorite things about our competition; they don't get it. In the people business—and that's what we're all in, not groceries, or car tires, or medicine; everybody is in customer service—people will pay extra, or travel out of their way, for convenience—and that means, *be quick!*"

Candace wrote as she listened:

23. Convenience = Profits

"I'll tell ya, ever since Mr. Walsh started doubling the deli staff, maybe fifteen years ago, Tony says the number of disgruntled customers has dropped to maybe ten percent of what it was."

"Ten percent! That's amazing. But he doubled the staff? Isn't that expensive?"

Roberta looked appraisingly at Candace. "You'd think so, but that's not how it plays out. What happened instead is, at first, sure, there were two clerks for every customer. There were lines only during our busiest times, and that was unavoidable—you just couldn't squeeze anyone else back there—but even *that* wasn't good enough for Mr. Walsh, so we extended the deli a yard or two, and stuck a few more guys back there.

"Well, lemme tell ya, people squawked. 'I can't believe how many guys are back there,' this and that; 'It's gotta be eating all of Walsh's profits,' 'He'll lose his shirt,' etc., etc. You get the picture."

Roberta paused for maximum effect. "Duh! No way! More people started coming here for their meats and cheeses, because they knew they'd be served right away. So, once they're in the store anyway, they figure, 'What the heck? Let's get everything else we need while we're here.' And guess who had to bust out a wall up front so they could put in six new registers?

"Was it all because of the deli being over-staffed? Who knows? All I know is, that's when Super Save closed its store across the street. They just couldn't compete anymore. Now there's something for your little notebook," Roberta said.

Candace opened a new page, and wrote:

> **24. Saving pennies on staffing will cost you dollars.**

* * * * *

Candace thought about that last one, Rule 24, because the concept was just so new to her: it defied conventional wisdom. Every company she'd studied in her business classes tortured the numbers to trim costs anywhere at all, and payroll was a favorite target of cost-cutters because it was such a huge piece of the pie. But here was Mr. Walsh, adding more cashiers and deli clerks rather than trying to make do with fewer. It seemed somehow hard to swallow. After all, her professors in business and economics weren't exactly dopes, and they would faint at this style of management.

To get a better handle on this one, she approached Ned, the general manager of one of the stores. She explained her conundrum, and Ned bought her a soda to drink while they discussed it.

"I had the same concern; a lot of us did. I remember talking about it with some of the other managers—I was still assistant store manager at the time—and we weren't so sure Bob's obsession with the customers' happiness really ought to go that far. Then one day Bob overhears some of us clucking like hens in a hen house, and he gathers us together to explain the numbers to us. This is the gist of that talk:

"'*What's the most expensive part of running a business?*' he asked us.

"'Rent,' one of us answered. 'Payroll,' said another. Inventory and advertising were also popular answers.

"'*All expensive, true,*' Bob said. '*You want my answer?*' He asked with that smirk of his. He knew we did! '*Our single biggest expense is in getting people through this door. Call it advertising, marketing, or whatever you like. It costs us more to attract new customers than any other thing we do. More than the rent we pay. More than the capital we've got tied up in all those jars and cans and tomatoes on the shelves. More than payroll, too. Sure, employing people is expensive—this is America, not China. But it's nothing compared to that one single biggest expense.*

"'*Including benefits for the full-timers, we pay our cashiers an average of $13 an hour. That means if we sell just four more watermelons, say, at one-hundred-percent mark-up, we've paid that person's wage. And you guys know the margins we make on a lot of our deli meat, and our cheese—gosh, two customers will cover the extra $19 we're paying to have one more full-time deli clerk on hand.*'

"He let that sink in. Some of us aren't so great at math, so it took us a minute," Ned joked. "Then Bob continued:

"'*If we hired more bodies and did the same volume in our store, then yeah, that would be throwing money away. But come on, you guys: you've seen our numbers; everyone on staff has. Are we doing the same volume now that we've increased the number of deli clerks and cashiers we have on hand?*'

"Let me tell you, Candace, that room was silent. Our payroll had increased immediately and dramatically, which was why we were all squawking in the first place: it caught our attention, and distracted us from two other numbers that were creeping higher and higher week after week. One was our volume: we were doing more business each week than at comparable weeks in years past. The other was our net profit. We were in uncharted territory, and it was looking great!

"I want people to come here, and I want them to come back. I want them to love us. I want them to tell all their friends, their neighbors, their coworkers, even strangers they meet in line at the bank, just how wonderful our store really is. I want them to brag about shopping here. To do all that, we can't just treat them well— we've got to spoil them rotten!"'

Ned and Candace shared a moment of silence. Candace thought she might finally be getting to the heart of what made Walsh's so spectacular. She opened up her notebook and wrote,

> **25. Getting new customers is a business' biggest expense. So do what it takes to keep them once they're yours.**

"So more payroll has led to more sales and greater profits," Candace said.

"Putting more people on the floor, to please our customers and make them want to come back, is exactly what we've done. We put more deli clerks on duty at any given time, and more people started coming to our deli. We sold more! And we did a lot better than just cover the extra wages we were paying—*a lot* better! So we'd have been crazy *not* to do it!"

"And most companies, most business leaders, are crazy."

"Well, now that I have a better understanding of this principle, I have a different term: short-sighted. Most companies— most managers—are penny wise, pound foolish. Customer service pays, and if you fail to see that, you're not much of a businessman—or woman."

Candace wrote another entry:

> **26. If you think payroll is expensive, try being understaffed.**

* * * * *

Mr. Walsh was due back from his trip in only two days. Candace really wanted to impress him upon his return, so she kept hard at work on her research. "What made Walsh's so special?" She asked everyone she could. "What do you guys do that other companies don't?"

One of those she asked was Mr. Franklin, a kind old retiree who had joined Walsh's as a bagger some years ago just for the fun of it—well, that and to supplement his "fixed income," which, as he put it, "Could use some fixing!"

"Mr. Franklin," Candace said as they each pushed a carriage back from the parking lot, "I've noticed you're never upset with your customers, even when you get an especially impolite one. Tell me how you do it."

"How I ...?"

"How you keep your spirits high and your smile wide, even when someone is miserable and wants you to be that way, too."

"Oh, that!" Mr. Franklin said. Candace had to walk slowly beside him, as he was getting on in years and wasn't all that speedy a walker. "I'd say the biggest hassle I get is for moving so slowly. 'Come on,' some people seem to be thinking. I get a lot of impatient sighs as I fill their trunks with groceries. 'Can't you work any faster?' I understand; I was young once, too. I was an executive for most of my career—something a lot of people fail to realize; that a bagger might have a better education and more experience than they do. But that's an aside. As I was saying: like some of our customers, I had the weight of the world on my shoulders for much of my youth—or I thought I did, anyway. A super-stressful job that helped me earn two divorces and one heart attack by age fifty. I had four kids, so I always fretted about their college tuition. One of my girls was always in trouble with boys, drugs, school, the law ... it took her a while to settle down." He looked around with exaggerated secrecy, and whispered, "Now she's an executive herself, by the way. Boy, if her kids, husband, boss, and PTA knew the half of it ...!"

Mr. Franklin paused. He smiled slyly. "Now, where was I? Bad kids ... troubles ... cranky customers.... Oh, there you go: how do I keep my spirits high? Well, that one's easy. I learned a game way back—Bob and the other long-time associates teach it to new hires, and we remind each other to play it all the time. We call it The Empathy Game. It goes like this: 'Maybe his kid just got her tongue pierced.'"

"I'm sorry," Candace said, blinking in disbelief. "You have a game about pierced tongues? Mr. Walsh taught it to you?"

Mr. Franklin laughed heartily. "Sounds nuts, doesn't it?"

"Um. Yes," Candace said, trying her best not to sound disrespectful.

"It may be nuts, but it's a great coping strategy. Say you are dealing with a customer who absolutely refuses to be nice, no matter what you do. He's snappy and impatient. He says something so rude, it seems as though he got out of bed this morning with the sole intention of ruining someone else's day, and he chose you. And there is nothing, try as you might, there is not one thing, that you can do to get him to come around."

Candace nodded but did not say a word. All she could think was, 'This from the company that taught me that the customer is always right, and if he's ever wrong, he's still right?'

Mr. Franklin gave Candace his widest smile yet. He seemed to read her thoughts on her face. "People are people, Candace, and even those of us who are usually nice can wake up on the wrong side of the bed from time to time. When we do, we're often tough to deal with. But our little game makes it all okay.

"The way the game works is that you say to yourself, when confronted by an especially irascible character, 'I know he seems like a jerk, but he's probably a nice guy, usually. He's just having a bad day, that's all. I'll bet his kid just got her tongue pierced. I should cut him a break.'

"You're young yet, Candace, so you may not fully appreciate this, but I'm here to tell you as a father, there would be few things worse than coming home from a long day's work only to find your ingrate punk of a sullen teenage daughter has an earring in her tongue. That'll set anyone off."

Now it was Candace's turn to laugh. "So if a customer is unpleasant, you make up an excuse for him."

"… And that makes it all easier to stomach. Sometimes we even end up feeling sorry for the unhappy S.O.B. It's important to remember that, while some people are just jerks, there are many who *do* have serious problems that we just don't know about. You have to feel bad for a guy whose wife is dying of cancer, for instance. It could take him a long time to come to terms with that. So this game isn't all sport; it also reminds us to be empathetic."

Mr. Franklin paused at that. He actually stopped pushing the carriage. It seemed to Candace that there might be more to his example than he was letting on. But it only took him a minute to cheer up again. He resumed walking.

"Of course, using the same explanation for each hateful customer wouldn't be all that fun or effective. The game is; what kind of a story can you make up for each person?"

"Like, Maybe her mother's in the hospital," Candace said.

"Good one!" replied Mr. Franklin. "Another one I like is, He has probably been stuck on a delayed plane all day, and he returned home to an empty fridge."

"Her ex-husband is probably a real jerk, and they just got off the phone," Candace said.

"Low blood sugar. Definitely low blood sugar. Poor dear," Mr. Franklin said, and shook his head dolefully.

Candace thought for a moment, then said, "I'll bet his car just got repossessed."

She and Mr. Franklin shared a laugh. Mr. Franklin said, "What pressure! His boss told him, 'Get the sale or get a new job.'"

Candace tried again: "She's got the stomach flu. And corns. Poor lady!"

"He's probably deathly afraid of crowds—what do they call that?"

"Agoraphobia."

"That's right! He's agoraphobic, and so he's nervous to be here, and this is his way of showing it."

"Good one," Candace said.

"Then again," Mr. Franklin said, "He probably just hates you."

They both got a good chuckle. Mr. Franklin entered the store as Candace wrote,

27. Play The Empathy Game.

* * * * *

Candace liked that talk with Mr. Franklin so much that she decided to keep digging on the topic of cranky customers. Her next mark was Gloria, in the courtesy booth.

"You've come to the right place," Gloria said. "We do three things here: sell lottery tickets, sell cigarettes, and handle complaints. We call ourselves the vice squad."

"So you'd say you get more than your share of cranky customers," Candace said.

"And then some! It's hard sometimes to remember that people *like* Walsh's, when all you meet are the ones who have a gripe.

"It could be a lot worse, though. I mean, at least we're here to help. I used to work in Customer Abuse at a retailer who shall remain nameless, and we weren't allowed to help anybody: 'You bought it, now it's yours!' was the unwritten policy."

"Customer Abuse. I like that," Candace said. "Tell me, Gloria; what do you do to stay nice when someone comes up to you with a downright vicious attitude?"

"Yeah, it happens, alright. I mean, most of our customers are very nice—I can't forget to mention that—but we have our share of monsters, too. That's why it's important for me to remember what one of my managers told me, when I'd just started: you should write this in your little book—it's become Gospel around here."

Candace did as she was told:

> **28. It's not you; it's the last guy.**

Candace looked perplexed. Gloria chided her: "Come on, college girl! The customer is on the offensive when she walks in the door. It's got nothing to do with you—"

"—It's because she was mistreated by so many others before you, she's expecting to be disappointed by you, too!" Candace jumped in.

"Now you're thinking," Gloria said. "That's exactly right. Think of how many times you've had a complaint—an overcharge on your credit card, the cable guy's late, you return a sweater only to find that you can only get store credit, and there's nothing there that you like; you complain about your meal, and not only does the waiter not care, but the manager isn't too sympathetic, either.... People are always letting us down!

"I'm a coffee maven—gotta have my Joe, and my doctor says at my age and weight, if I use creamer, I'm not going to meet my grandkids. So I always ask for milk. Half of the places I go, though, don't have it—it's half and half or nothing—or they'll *sell* you milk separately, if you want it. It's for coffee, for cripe's sake! I want to yell. Whenever I walk into some fast food joints now—they're the worst at it—I'm already spoiling for a fight."

"I see," Candace said. "So you're feeling kinda nasty even before someone says, 'May I help you?' because you've been let down so many times before."

Gloria nodded proudly. "You got it, Candace. Now, how can I be mad at someone for starting out nasty, when they're just acting the way any sensible person would act: ready for conflict?" Gloria winked. "The fun part is turning them into friends. At Walsh's, we don't let our customers down. I can't tell you the last time one of my customers left this booth still mad. Most of the time, they love us more than ever, because we routinely do what no one else seems able—or at least willing—to do: we solve problems."

* * * * *

Candace liked Rule #28. But she wanted another perspective before Mr. Walsh returned. So she asked the bakery manager, Ethan, for his take on cranky customers.

"That's easy," Ethan replied. "Repeat after me: 'I know exactly how frustrated you must feel!' Say it like you mean it—because if you work here and your customer is unhappy, you *do* mean it."

"That's a good one," Candace said, getting out her notebook. Ethan held his hand over the book, stopping her from writing.

"I mean it, Candi," he said. Candace laughed inwardly. No one had called her Candi since her grandfather had passed away.

"Repeat after me," he continued. "'I know …'"

"I know exactly how frustrated you must feel," Candace said, chuckling at his insistence.

Ethan shrugged. "Hey, you want to manage, you have to know how to teach. And practice is the best way for your student to learn.

"Now, expressing your feelings isn't all of it. You have to follow up with action. To do that, we'll say something like, 'I'm sure there's something we can do to make this right.' Then we do whatever it takes. We don't let anyone walk away dissatisfied, no matter how inconvenient it might be to help them."

Candace liked it: Walsh's associates were taught to disarm cranky customers through empathy and action. Something bad happened to you? Then you're ready for a fight: that's Rule #28. Walsh's associates let you know that they are *at least* as horrified with what happened as you are. Candace collected variations on Ethan's two phrases from across the company. This is what she wrote:

29. Disarm Cranky Customers.

First, say ...

> "I know exactly how you must feel."
>
> "I am *so* sorry that happened to you."
>
> "That's terrible!"

Follow up with ...

> "I'm sure there's something we can do to make this right."
>
> "We'll get this fixed in a jiffy."
>
> "This is an easy problem to solve."
>
> "We'll straighten this out; that's what I'm here for."
>
> "I'm not going to give up until you're completely Delighted."
>
> "Helping you is why I woke up this morning."
>
> "Don't worry: you're in good hands now."
>
> "My job is to spoil you. How can I do that?"

* * * * *

As Ethan pointed out to Candace a little later, "The thing is, Candi, it *is* awful when something bad happens here at Walsh's. So there's nothing cheesy to this at all. I won't have a customer who is anything but Delighted! Not at my store."

"I believe you, Ethan. I can tell that's the ethic of the company. But what do you do *in particular* to solve a customer's problem?"

"Get out your pen, and I'll spell it out. Then I'll walk you through it."

Candace did as she was told. She wrote,

> **30. Handling Complaints**
>   1) **Listen—then listen some more.**
>   2) **Say, "I'm sorry"—and mean it.**
>   3) **Say, "What can I do to make it right?" Do it.**
>   4) **Follow up**

"Really, there are thirteen steps to fixing a complaint, but this Reader's Digest version will get you started," Ethan said. "First and foremost, you've got to listen. People don't listen enough. So what you're really going to do is alternate listening and apologizing until they've gotten it off their chest. A lot of people just need a sympathetic ear, you know: often, after a good venting, they're all set. Go figure." He shrugged.

"The other thing about listening is that it's just plain tacky to fix the wrong complaint. That's a two-star mistake at best. So a big part of the listening step is to rephrase their complaint in your own words. That does two things. First, it shows them you care, that you were actually paying attention. Anyone can parrot back what they just heard, but when you rephrase it, the other person knows you actually heard them.

"The second thing rephrasing does is, it lets them correct you. For instance, someone says, 'My fish wasn't cut the way I like it, and the guy who took my order had a bad attitude.' What is the customer's complaint?"

"A poorly-cut fish," Candace replied.

"If you give him an apology and a new piece cut just the way he likes it, he's going to go home mad, and tell all his friends what surly help we have here at Walsh's. It's the attitude of the fish guy that has this customer angry, not the way he sliced his portions. When you rephrase the customer's words—'Your fish wasn't cut properly, sir?'—he has a chance to correct you with something like, 'No, stupid! I said the guy was rude!'"

"Do many people call you stupid, Ethan?" Candace asked. Boy, she thought, if someone mistreated her like that ...!

Ethan laughed. "I've been called some bad things, yeah. It's actually kinda funny. I mean really, who raises these people? If I ever treated someone like that, my mom would send me to my room without dinner—and I'm forty-one! Oh, well. All I can say in a case like that is, This poor guy's daughter probably just—"

"—had her tongue pierced," Candace finished for him. "I like that one."

Ethan got a good laugh out of that. "I was going to say that she got pregnant, dropped out of high school, stole her dad's motorcycle, and rode off to Vegas with her boyfriend."

"No wonder he's upset!" Candace said. They both giggled some more.

"Moving on," Ethan continued. "The next step is saying you're sorry. That's pretty clear, though again, people don't do it sincerely enough.

"It's the third step that I love best, though: Ask how you can make it right."

"Don't you just fix the problem and give them a freebee, to show you're sincerely sorry? I've noticed a lot of that around the store, especially free coffees."

"You're one step ahead. When someone has a complaint, you can rack your brain and think of a terrific way to compensate them, or you can let *them* do the work by suggesting what you

can do to fix their gripe. That second option has several especially powerful qualities.

"For one, the solution is their idea, so whatever you end up
giving, they're bound to be happy—you're giving them what
they asked for!

"For another, this question stops people dead in their tracks.
Nobody asks a customer what it would take to make them
happy again. Even at a nice restaurant, when your order is
botched somehow, what do they do? They might comp. your
meal, so it's free, or they might give you a dessert on the house.
But that's automatic; it's the same for everyone, and the manager got that out of a playbook. With our 'What can I do …?'
question, we've gone a step further than anyone else our customers encounter. They like that.

"And here's the last one. Before instituting this question, we
used to give away more free product than we do now!'

"What? How could that be?" Candace asked.

"Simple. People are honest. Nobody wants to take advantage of
you (next to nobody, anyway). You tell them they can have whatever they want, and nine times out of ten, they're going to say, 'Oh,
no. I'm all set.' They're grateful you asked, and you're done.

"… Except that we still give them something. Naturally, we
fix the original problem; I hope that goes without saying. But
when they say 'nothing,' that's when we throw in a little extra—
a coffee, a small bouquet of flowers, a pint of Ben & Jerry's, or
something else."

"That tenth guy. What do you do with him?" Candace asked.

"Usually, what he suggests is cheaper than what we used to give away, anyway. So we give it to him, he's happy, and so are we."

Candace pondered that a moment before asking, "And following up?"

"Follow up is simple: Either Bob or one of the store managers calls the customer later that day or early the next, and asks how things turned out. People love to hear from the top dog—they're so flattered! It's funny, but even hot-shot executives pulling down mid-six figure salaries are honored and impressed when they get this call. That is the five-star icing on the cake. Without that phone call, it's just not the same. We might still lose 'em as customers. But you do that last step, and they'll tell all their friends. They're your great buddy next time they're in, and for years afterwards. We showed them we care, and they're grateful. We've earned their loyalty."

* * * * *

Mr. Walsh returned from his trip completely invigorated, recharged after a week of travel with his wife.... Not that he had ever seemed to lack energy or drive before, of course. Candace was amazed that a man of his years could have so much more pep than she, when she was still in college!

As soon as he had a chance, he grabbed Candace from her duty—she was helping the maintenance guys by washing the floors—and told her to sit down for one of their chats. In his hand was a plain brown Walsh's bag, stuffed with papers, notebooks, and who knew what else. He placed it on the chair beside him.

"You wouldn't believe the things I've seen!" Mr. Walsh said. "Judy and I—Mrs. Walsh—hit different cities, stayed in different hotels, ate in a wide selection of restaurants, and (my favorite) we shopped at quite a number of different stores, including grocery stores, from big chains to one-shot deals and all in between. Do you know what we found?"

"No," Candace said.

"We found that no one does what we do: as far as we can tell, companies don't spend any time studying other businesses for fresh new ideas! Not even the ones right next door to them."

Mr. Walsh shook his head. "It's just amazing. Here's an example. Whenever we're within a hundred miles of Southern Connecticut, Judy and I head off to Westport and Norwalk, to visit two companies that nail five-star service cold. One is Stew Leonard's—"

"The World's Largest Dairy Store," Candace said proudly. "Rule number two."

"Exactly. Gosh, there's so much to learn from those guys. And right up the Post Road in Westport is this simply amazing store, Mitchells."

"Jack Mitchell wrote *Hug Your Customers*. It's a great book!"

Mr. Walsh looked at Candace appraisingly. "You are a sharp student," he said.

"School library," she said. "My professor recommended I read it as soon as I told her about my research project on Walsh's."

"Hmn," murmured Mr. Walsh. Then, reaching into his plain brown Walsh's bag, he drew out a copy of that book. "Here's your own copy, autographed by the author himself."

Candace accepted the gift with reverence. The present itself mattered to her far less than the fact that Mr. Walsh had thought of her while on his trip.

"Thank you so much," she said, somewhat awed.

"It's entirely my pleasure," he said—and they shared a laugh, as that was his favorite line.

"So here's the thing. Right there, within twenty minutes of each other, are two of the most remarkable stores in all of retail.

One is ultra-expensive, and always busy. (That alone is a lesson for you). The other is extremely competitive on price, and also incredibly busy."

"That's right," Candace said. "I've researched both. The Mitchell family has two very upscale stores, and they do $65 million in sales a year. Stew Leonard's has three stores that are fiercely competitive on price, and they do $300 million a year. Two very different business models; both amazing."

Mr. Walsh raised an eyebrow at his pupil, but didn't comment otherwise. He didn't have to—the sign let Candace know how impressed he was. She blushed—something she found herself doing a lot around Mr. Walsh, who was so free with his heartfelt compliments.

"Yes," he said, "and the story continues. With these two remarkable companies to learn from, you would expect other businesses in the area to have picked up their tricks decades ago. But not so! I won't bother to elaborate on the cruddy, all-too-average service we experienced in other supermarkets within a short drive of Stew Leonard's, or the lame effort put out by other haberdashers near Mitchells."

"Haberdashers," Candace said teasingly.

"That word kills me," Mr. Walsh replied. "What a strange, wonderful language we have." He paused, collected his thoughts, and then proceeded.

"The next day, we were off to New Jersey, where we found my favorite store in all the world: Wegmans."

"Sixty-five stores from Rochester, New York down to D.C." Candace remarked. "$3.8 billion last year. Fortune's Best Company to Work For in 2005, second best in 2006, and third best in 2007. They pretty much live at the top of that list year in, year out."

Mr. Walsh smiled again. "And, if you ever start a business of your own, the first thing you should do is exactly what Mrs. Walsh and I did the year before we opened our first store: rent a home within a short drive of a few of their stores, and shop there every day. Talk to people. Make friends. Experience business exactly as it should be done."

"A business of my own?" Candace asked. "Any business? Not just a grocery store?"

Mr. Walsh laughed heartily. "Any dope who thinks she can't learn vital best practices from *all* industries doesn't deserve a business of her own. I've studied industries as diverse as manufacturing, insurance, healthcare … we're all in customer service, Candace, and we can learn something from everyone.

"But especially from a five-star company such as Wegmans.

"So, when we started Walsh's, my very first step was to emulate everything they did in our own store. Every last thing! I decided, well, it's clear that they're the best: across industries, Wegmans provides the highest level of Customer Delight while still operating at a cost-competitive rate. So, they're the mark to beat. And you can't beat someone till you've matched them.

"To this day, every time Wegmans turns left, so do we. They turn right, we turn right. They back up, we usually do, too.

"That's what I don't get about companies in any field: If you want the best results, do what the best in your field does—*especially* in your field, even though, as I said, you should learn from everyone you can. Why GM and Ford don't mimic Toyota and Honda, I'll never understand! I still can't believe that *twice* now, they've let the Japanese take the lead on fuel efficiency, once in the seventies, again now with hybrids and other eco-conscious technology."

Mr. Walsh paused, seeming to catch himself. "But that's its own book right there, isn't it? Let's get back to my area of expertise: Customer Delight. Now where was I?"

Candace marveled at the energy of her mentor; she found it endearing that he got ahead of himself and forgot the way back sometimes. "Copying the best," she said. "You were saying—"

"Got it. It's imperative you copy everything the best does; you can't pick and choose on that, either. Do ninety percent, you're still ten percent behind. Better write that down, Candace."

Candace did:

> 31. To match the best, you have to do every-
> thing that the best does. So study and
> copy the best. (Inside of your field, but in
> other industries as well).

"You'll never be as good as the best through mimicry, though—there's only one best, after all, and to merely copy someone else … well, what copy is as good as the original? So modeling your company after the established leader is a starting point, that's all. I knew that if I was going to make Walsh's the greatest supermarket in the world, I would have to search for practices to surpass the current leaders in ways that they haven't even thought of."

"I think I should write that down, too," Candace said, and wrote:

> **32. To beat the best, improve on what they do.**

Mr. Walsh read over her shoulder, nodding. "Exactly. To beat the best, this is when I started studying other companies as well. Getting back to Stew Leonard's, the way the Leonard Family runs their stores, for example, is brilliant! They offer an awful lot of products these days, but they only sell things that they get at a special price. One time you go there, Cheerios are fifty cents below any other store. The next time, there are no Cheerios at all."

"I've noticed you do that here. Isn't that frustrating to your shoppers?"

"If they came here looking for everything, then yes, they'd be frustrated. But Walsh's shoppers come into our store knowing three things: One, we've got the best selection of meat, fish, cheese, and fresh vegetables and fruit on the planet—every time. When Super Save is selling those Styrofoam so-called tomatoes you get most places, ours are practically still warm from the sun—yes, even mid-winter. Everything on the perimeter of the store is the best you can buy, without exception.

"Two, the center-aisle stuff is hit or miss, but it's always priced way below what other stores charge. Our shoppers are savvy. 'Come for the fruit, and come back for the bargains.' That was one of our ad campaigns, probably before you were born."

Candace waited, but it seemed that Mr. Walsh was done. Finally, she spoke up. "You said there was one more thing your shoppers know when they come here."

Mr. Walsh laughed. "You caught me: I did! Sorry, I was thinking about my trip. The third thing…. Oh, yeah. We treat 'em right. We spoil 'em rotten. A Walsh customer may not be all that important out in the real world: maybe his boss dumps on him all week long, his wife doesn't give him the time of day, his kids think he's a relic. But for an hour once a week, he's the center of the universe. We treat each and every customer as if he spends a million dollars in our store each week." He was clearly proud of himself. "I like that. Add it to your book."

> **33. Treat every customer like they spend $1 million a week with your company.**

"You know the 80/20% Rule?" Mr. Walsh asked.

"The Paredo Principle. It's originally a math concept, but in business it means that twenty percent of your customers account for eighty percent of your sales. So most businesses focus on that twenty percent of VIPs, and don't worry as much about the rest."

"Paredo, huh? Good job once again, Candace."

"Much obliged," Candace said with a smile.

"There's only one part of that they forget to teach you in business school: It's a bunch of bull!"

Candace's grin shriveled instantly.

"80/20% only works because companies ignore the potential of that less-enthusiastic majority. Sure, any business has a core 20% that sustains the bulk of its sales. That, as your Mr. Paredo suggests, is a fact of nature.

"But since when did Mankind accept what Mother Nature handed us, without trying to improve upon it? We don't live in caves, and there's no reason we should be passive with our customers, either."

"Caves …"

"It's like this, Candace. Every business has this huge, under-utilized eighty percent that *could* bring a whole ton more profits, if only company leadership would try to woo them! Here at Walsh's, we don't accept that twenty percent of our customers are VIPs, and that's as good as it'll ever get. Think about it: every person that shops in here is looking for about the same number of calories per week for her family."

"Calories. I'd never thought of it that way," Candace said, but Mr. Walsh seemed hardly to notice; he was on a roll.

"If twenty percent of our shoppers are buying eighty percent of the calories we sell, that means that the other eighty percent of shoppers are buying most of their calories elsewhere—we're sharing their wallets with our competition! What kind of moronic businessman would just sit around and let that go on, right under his nose, without trying to do something about it?"

Candace had to jump in; this seemed a bit simplistic for her liking.

"But Mr. Walsh," she said. "Some of your customers are bigger buyers because of their situation. A bigger family. A larger household budget. Some people hold dinner parties every week, and some never do. Some people eat like birds; others ... not so much."

"All true. There are certainly individual differences among our customers that explain their buying habits, and some of that stuff—like budget, social life, eating habits—we're not going to change. I'm with you.

"However, when you look at a large enough population, as we can with our thousands of customers in our different towns, these differences fade a bit. Share of wallet, though: that doesn't fade. People who give us all their shopping dollars are the foundation of our business. I want a bigger foundation! I want more share of wallet.

"That's why we treat every customer the same: like she's the only customer we'll have all week. If you only had one customer, wouldn't you be sure to spoil her?"

"Sure! Otherwise, I'd go broke."

"Absolutely, Candace. So that's one of our not-so-secret secrets of success: we spoil everyone, from the guy in here buying a lottery ticket and newspaper, to the mother of six who drops $250 every Thursday, year after year.

"After all, who's to say that the lottery guy hasn't got *ten* kids at home? Maybe he'll win that lottery, and he'll call us for our home-cooked catering every night for the rest of his life. I want to be the one he buys everything from, not just a lottery ticket and newspaper.

"Spoil 'em Rotten, Candace."

Candace nodded. "I think I have my next lesson." She wrote,

> **34. Spoil 'em all, and get more share of wallet. (Instead of 80/20%, why not 100/100%?)**

Mr. Walsh read over her shoulder and said, "You're a quick study, that's for sure. Keep up the good work." And with that, he was off, leaving Candace in his wake.

* * * * *

"Mr. Walsh, I've learned a tremendous amount about Customer Delight since you took me under your wing. You and your associates have given me perspective on the philosophy behind customer service—"

"Attitude."

"Yes, you've taught me about the attitude necessary to deliver that top one-percent of service again and again.

"You've taught me lessons about leading a Five-Star Customer Service organization—"

Mr. Walsh interrupted again: "Leadership is essential to the effort. That's why most companies never come close to that Five-Star level. If your leaders don't get Customer Delight, there's no way your whole company will. At best, it's hit or miss throughout the ranks."

"What's your expression for that one again? Something about stinky fish …?"

Mr. Walsh chuckled. "It's my favorite quote on leadership. It's worth writing down."

> **35. A fish stinks from the head. Whenever you receive bad customer service, look all the way to the CEO. It's his fault.**

"Of course, the same goes for great customer service. If a whole company is doing something right, it's because the CEO gets it. If a particular division is performing well, it's because the division manager gets it. If a store or branch or hotel gives Delightful service, it's because the general manager gets it. If a shift gives great service—"

"… It's because the shift leader knows what Customer Delight is all about," Candace finished, feeling quite proud.

"You got it, sister! A stinky fish—the organization—smells that way because of its leader, its 'head.' But fish heads make outstanding fertilizer, too. If the leader wants, he can be the source of customer service, instead of the source of stench."

"Fertilizer," Candace said dubiously.

Mr. Walsh laughed in his endearing, self-deprecating way. "Okay, you caught me. I tortured that analogy a bit. But I don't have a good line for how the leader doesn't have to stink. I'm forced to make do."

They shared a hearty chuckle. Candace was still astonished that a man of Mr. Walsh's stature and accomplishment would be so convivial, so … *human.* She treasured their friendship. After a minute, she continued with her point.

"What I'm trying to get at, Mr. Walsh, is that I've learned a lot about Customer Delight in my time here, but my education thus far seems to be piecemeal: a little of this, a bit of that. What ties all of your practices and philosophy together?"

Mr. Walsh raised his eyebrows, a look of pleasant surprise on his face. After allowing himself a minute of reflection, he said, "You've really stumped me with that one. I'm going to have to give it some thought. 'What is behind everything we do here at Walsh's?' Hmn.... Good question."

He ruminated some more. For Candace, the silence actually became uncomfortable. Finally, Mr. Walsh spoke up.

"Tomorrow. Give me tonight to sleep on your question. The learning begins again in the morning. See you at six?"

Inwardly, Candace groaned: Six?! College kids weren't supposed to wake up before noon! And when Mr. Walsh said six, she knew he'd be looking for her starting at five-thirty. Oh, well, she thought. Nothing is too much for Mr. Walsh.

"Six it is, Captain!" she said with a smile.

Mr. Walsh smiled back. "There's another lesson right there, Candace, one that you've got down cold. In Customer Delight, the answer is always "Yes! Now, what's the question?"

Candace took dictation:

> **36. "Yes! Now what is the question?"**

"That one lesson alone, Candace, is worth more than your parents paid for your four years of college."

With that, Mr. Walsh was off to shake hands and kiss babies.

The next morning, Candace was there before Mr. Walsh. She was now so familiar with everyone in the store that the manager of the night crew, Mark, unlocked the door to let her in—not his usual way of doing business. Candace took her extra time to make a fresh pot of coffee, for which Mark's whole staff was grateful. She didn't drink coffee herself, but she poured Mr. Walsh a cup and prepared it exactly the way he liked it. When he finally arrived, at ten of six, Candace and his coffee were waiting for him.

"S.O.P." he said by way of greeting. He took the proffered cup with a warm nod of thanks. "The first of the three-part answer to your question is, S.O.P."

"Standard Operating Procedure," Candace said. "You take the behaviors you want everyone to practice, and you standardize them, turning them into rules so that everyone knows what is expected."

"Well, the word 'rules' is over-stating it a bit," Mr. Walsh replied. "Are you familiar with the Nordstrom Code?"

"I'm a Marshall's girl myself," Candace said.

"And well you should be: no one's going to know where you got your Donna Karan sweater, so why pay full price? But here's the Nordstrom Code:"

> **37. The Nordstrom Code:**
> **Use good judgment in all situations.**
> **There will be no additional rules.**

"I like it!" Candace said. "Before starting here, I would've thought that was impossible: my impression of most managers is, they'd tell you that if you trusted your employees to use their heads rather than their handbooks, the whole company would disintegrate in a day!"

"But you've noticed something different is possible here at Walsh's, haven't you?"

"You live by the Nordstrom Code, don't you, Mr. Walsh?"

"I didn't invent customer service, Candace. When I come across a trick that works somewhere else, we adopt it without hesitation. Nordstrom is a phenomenal company, with a top-rate reputation. They hire competent adults, and give them the freedom to use their talent for the benefit of the customer—and the stockholders.

"There's a flip side to the Nordstrom Code, you know. Got your pen handy?"

Candace held it up, poised for action.

> **38. If you treat your associates like children, guess how they'll act?**

"That's why SOP isn't a list of rules made to be strictly enforced. Instead, it's a collection of practices that we encourage. *Strongly* encourage, mind you. But we prefer the carrot to the stick around here."

Candace stood there, ready to take more notes—to finally dive into Mr. Walsh's lesson on Standard Operating Procedures. It wasn't to be, however. In the blink of an eye he was off, unlocking the front door and greeting his staff as they filed in. Everyone beamed as they greeted him back. Walsh's associates clearly adored their fearless leader, and it was plain to see that they were tickled that he would hold the door for them.

* * * * *

It was lunchtime before Candace was again alone with Mr. Walsh. One minute, she was stocking olives on a shelf in aisle nine; the next, Mr. Walsh was the one doing the stocking, while Candace stood, notebook in hand, pen at the ready. What other business owner would get on his knees so a worker could take notes? Nothing Mr. Walsh did surprised Candace any more.

"S.O.P., Candace. It's how Marriott got to be the biggest hotelier in the world without compromising on quality. When you discover a behavior that Delights your Customers, standardize it. Spread the word. Get everyone doing it. It'll raise the level of service throughout the entire organization."

Mr. Walsh paused in his work and looked up at his protégé.

"'This is how we do it here.' Have you heard any of our associates say that, Candace?"

"Sure have, Mr. Walsh. Also its opposite: 'We don't do that here at Walsh's,'" she replied.

Mr. Walsh nodded as he got back to work. As he placed each jar, he made sure it was lined up perfectly, for maximum aesthetic impact. Candace played one of his favorite lines in her head: 'The customer eats with her eyes.' He would explain every chance he got: 'When she shops for food, she's thinking with her eyes, which are connected directly to her stomach. Show her you care, and that you're proud of your store. When things look nice, you'll tantalize your customers and sell more food. It's simple as that.'

"We've got our own S.O.P. divided into three areas," he continued. "Seven All-Associate Behaviors, seven we'll call Process, and one Manager Behavior. These fifteen points are the backbone of our operations—our minimum, if you will. If we just get these few things down pat across the board, we'll be way ahead of almost any other company out there."

He stopped for effect.

"Candace, there's something that is tragically overlooked by almost every company in business today. Write down a new lesson for me, would you?"

Candace did as she was told:

> **39. Get everyone doing your SOPs. *Everyone.*
> All the time.**

Mr. Walsh looked at what Candace had written. "You know, it drives me nuts, but there is almost no company out there that actually follows lesson number thirty-nine. It's just incredible! I could single one or two, but what would be the point of that? So many companies have great practices on the books, but so few actually *use* those terrific ideas ..." He shook his head in wonder. "What's the matter with managers these days, Candace? This stuff is so darned easy!"

Candace knew this was a rhetorical question. Mr. Walsh didn't expect an answer, and that was just as well. Candace had no idea why people didn't use the great ideas that their companies' training departments had available to them.

Mr. Walsh continued: "Here's the trick to making the previous rule work for any company: you can't just standardize everything and expect your staff to fall into line. You have to choose some basics which represent your bare minimum—the SOPs that are most important to your particular company. They should be big ones, noticeable to your customers, if they are to have maximum impact."

"So," Candace said, "If rule number thirty-nine entails creating a hundred SOPs, rule forty tells you to choose just a few that matter the most."

"Exactly," Mr. Walsh said. "Ready to write?"

Candace nodded her assent, and held her pen at the ready.

40. Create your own "Core" SOPs

Walsh's "Core 15"

All-Associate Behaviors
1) Just Say Yes!
2) 15/5 Rule
3) Use Their Names
4) "My Pleasure"
5) Take Them To The Item Every Time
6) "See Ya Soon"
7) "Enjoy Your Next Coffee On Us"

Process
1) Answer phone in two rings *or fewer.*
2) Avoid stocking shelves while the store is open.
3) Patrol the aisles.
4) 2 to a checkout line—*MAX!*
5) Carryout service (Standard. No tipping).
6) Continue the sale next week.
7) Forgot your wallet? You can pay next time.

Management
1) Top two managers visible and engaged with customers during peak hours.

"Now, here's the thing with our Core 15, Candace: this stuff is all very specific to Walsh's." He thought about that a moment, then said, "Well, that's not entirely true. Any grocer would be wise to follow these SOPs. Some of the 15, like the 15/5 Rule for instance, are good ideas for any company. But a lot of this is what we choose as *our* Core 15. Another company might have its own Core 15—or ten, or nineteen. So I'm not sure how this is going to help you with your term paper."

Candace looked at Mr. Walsh as if he were crazy. She caught herself and tried to wipe the look off her face. "Mr. Walsh!" she said emphatically. "You don't see how your Core 15 carries over? I'll tell you how: you explain how each point works for you. Other managers in different companies can take your specific example and generalize it. So go ahead, give it to me: How does each of these fifteen work? And why do you do it?"

"You want it, you got it, Candace. Let's dive in after lunch. I'm starved." Mr. Walsh replied.

'Oh no!' Candace thought. But she was getting used to Mr. Walsh interrupting their sessions together. He didn't like to force too much information on her at a single time. He'd tell her something, then let it soak in a while, then give her a new lesson, let it simmer.... Plus, he couldn't stand to be away from the hustle and bustle of his store for too long; he had to interact with his customers and associates often, or, Candace thought fondly, he might explode.

★ ★ ★ ★ ★

They enjoyed a terrific Reuben sandwich, cooked up in the store's kitchen as one of the day's specials. While they ate, Candace and Mr. Walsh spoke mostly with associates, who were completely comfortable coming up to the Big Boss with a question, a suggestion, or a friendly word. Candace admired that about her older friend.

After lunch, Mr. Walsh told Candace to open her notebook again.

"Let's jump back into this Core 15 thing. We'll number them as regular lessons for your notes, now that we've identified them as Core. And we'll only do one at a time, because there's a lot of work to do around the store today. We'll work a little, talk a little, all day long. Ready? Here goes."

41. Just Say Yes!

"This is one of my all-time favorites—that's why I put it first. In Customer Delight, our job is to say, "Yes!" to our customers' requests, if at all humanly possible. If an associate doesn't know, they are to find out: 'I don't know' isn't an option. And, only a manager can say No."

"Seriously?"

"Seriously. 'No' is the ugliest word in our language. I don't want just anybody getting ugly with our customers." Mr. Walsh laughed, and Candace knew why. To him, none of his people was 'just anybody.' To Mr. Walsh, every person on his payroll was a very important somebody.

"Another consideration, which I guess you could say is an added bonus of this SOP, is that nobody wants to have to tell a customer No—who wants to be the bearer of bad news? So, by restricting No to the managers, you're removing one of the worst aspects of a person's job. I guess you could call it a fringe benefit for our associates. We pay the managers the big bucks because we expect them to do the dirty work.

"Now let's move on," Mr. Walsh said, "There's a lot to cover."

Candace poised her pen over the paper, ready to record the next tip.

"… Just as soon as we talk to my old friend Henry Swartz over there. He's been in here every week since we first opened in 1981. We've catered each of his four daughters' weddings. Judy and I love the Swartzes."

This really is going to take all day, isn't it? Candace thought with a sigh as she followed in Mr. Walsh's wake.

* * * * *

Twenty minutes later, Mr. Walsh asked Candace to open her book again.

42. Observe the 15/5 Rule

"Again, this isn't a rule, just a good idea that I want everyone to practice," said Mr. Walsh with a twinkle in his eye. Nobody laughed at himself more than Mr. Walsh, Candace had learned.

"When do you say hello to someone standing nearby, or walking past? When do you smile, or nod, or wave? This takes away all of the guess work.

"When a person—customer or staffer—is between five and fifteen feet of you, you give them a non-verbal sign of acknowledgement: a smile, nod, etc. When they're within five feet of you, you say something, such as Hello, Good morning, or How are you? In order to show you recognize their humanity."

"Doesn't that take a lot of the spontaneity out of it?" Candace asked.

"Not at all. It gives you permission to be nice. Let's face it, different people have different upbringings, different levels of friendliness, different levels of shyness … I want everyone, no matter how shy or how much of a Yankee, to know that it's okay to be warm. Not just okay, either: it's *expected*. We've found that our associates love it, *especially* the shy ones. Our customers love it, too. We hear it all the time: Walsh's is the friendliest place in town. This is one big reason why."

Mr. Walsh checked his watch. "Time for a snack. I understand that we're sampling hot apple pie in the bakery. We can resume after that. Gotta set your priorities, you know!"

* * * * *

"What's next on the list?" Mr. Walsh asked as they sat down to enjoy what was probably the most delicious apple pie Candace had ever tasted. She read from her list,

43. Use Their Names

"People love the sound of their own names," said Mr. Walsh. "It's one of the most important lessons you can learn from Dale Carnegie, and he's got a lot of important lessons to teach."

"How to Win Friends and Influence People," Candace said. "It's a classic."

"Sure is. So here at Walsh's, we often just ask our customers what their name is. I got that idea from Starbucks. When you order a coffee, they'll ask what name they should put on your cup, so they can call you when it's ready. That way, the partners, as their associates are called, are ready to greet you with, "Hi, Candace!" the next time you come in. It's a little trick that goes a long way toward making the customer feel special—and that's a fundamental part of Customer Delight."

"I noticed that at Starbucks, they use first names when they do that. Even older customers are Bill and Mary, not Mr. or Mrs.. What's your take on that?"

Mr. Walsh seemed pleased with Candace's query. "When I was a boy, kids were taught to use surnames to show respect for our elders. At work, subordinates would call the boss Mr. Smith or what have you, and Mr. Smith would call you Bob, or maybe Walsh, with no Mr. It kinda put people in their place. Doctors pulled the same stunt—many still do, even though I'm older than my doctors by now.

"It's a bunch of bull, Candace. Life changed for most of us in the Seventies. My kids, who were pretty young back then, called my friends by their first names, even though my friends included business leaders, state office holders, and the like.

"At Mitchells, clerks all use first names. They do it intentionally to establish themselves as peers, one professional to another. I think it's a point well taken."

"But I'm sure most of Jack Mitchell's sales staffers are middle-aged and make six figures, just like many of his customers; maybe they *are* peers. When you have a sixteen-year-old bagger—"

"Or a twenty-one-year-old college kid?" Mr. Walsh asked. It was clear from his demeanor that he was only having some fun with her.

"Well, yes, sir. What should I call you? I was raised to show a certain amount of respect to my elders …"

"And I think that's great!" Mr. Walsh replied. "This is a matter of personal comfort. I'm not about to tell my associates what to call our customers. If you're comfortable being deferential, go for it. If it makes you feel more at ease to be familiar, that works, too. It's up to you."

"So I can keep calling you Mr. Walsh?"

"Absolutely. And if Bob works for you at some point, you can switch. I won't hold it against you."

"Uh, thank you, Mr.—Bob," Candace stammered.

Mr. Walsh laughed. "Mr. Bob was a clay figure on Saturday Night Live. Best stick with Mr. Walsh for now."

Candace was pretty sure the hapless clay man was Mr. *Bill,* not Bob, but she let it go.

They had finished their pie. Without a word, Mr. Walsh took both of their paper plates and threw them away. He kept right on walking, signaling for Candace to follow him.

* * * * *

"Okay, what's next?" Mr. Walsh asked as they headed toward the back of the store.

"The next of your Core 15 is 'My pleasure,'" Candace said.

"Already covered. Next?"

44. Take Them To The Item Every Time

"This is such an important part of what we do here!" Mr. Walsh said emphatically. "Too many people think that helping the customer interrupts their work. What a bunch of bunk! Helping the customer *is* our work! All of those other tasks are what we do to keep busy in the down time between when our customers need us."

"That's something I've never thought of before," Candace said.

"No one has! Better write that in your book."

> **45. Helping the customer doesn't interrupt our work; it *is* our work!**

"The way this plays out, then, is that we drop everything for a customer. We help them, and that includes walking them to the item they've requested: absolutely! And not just sometimes, or usually; we do this *every single time!*" Mr. Walsh was practically shaking, he felt so strongly about this one. "If I see an associate pointing the way for a customer, there's hell to pay!"

"Up with that you will not put!" Candace said.

Mr. Walsh stopped and chuckled. "I see you're a Churchill fan, too. Bottom line, if a customer wants to know where something is, we take her there. Every single time, no matter what we're doing at the time—though, of course, a cashier can't leave his post. In that case, he'll call over the front-end manager to help."

"Gotcha," Candace said.

Their walk had brought them to the loading dock out back. A huge pile of boxes lay beside the double doors. "Let's lend a hand and crush some boxes for the recycling truck, shall we?"

"Sounds like fun!" Candace said.

"Oh, there are few things more cathartic than stepping on corrugated cardboard to take out the day's frustrations. Let's do it!"

* * * * *

"Okay, Champ, what's forty-six?" Mr. Walsh asked after they had finished crushing boxes.

"Next, we have the Walsh version of, 'Have a nice day.'"

46. "See Ya Soon"

Mr. Walsh explained. "We talked earlier about how 'You're welcome' is vanilla; we don't even notice it any more. It's the same with 'Have a nice day.' Nobody even notices when you say it. Sometimes, it's so clearly insincere that people are actually turned off by it.

"Remember, in every exchange we have with a customer, we have three options: turn them off, make no impression at all, or leave them feeling special."

"So Ethan told me," Candace interjected.

"Ethan's a sharp cookie," Mr. Walsh said. He continued with his explanation. "Saying Goodbye is one of the last things they experience with us; first and last impressions are the most important, aren't they?"

"Primacy and recency," Candace agreed. "They're what people remember."

"Of course they are," he agreed. "When we say, 'See you soon,' or—even better with a regular customer whose routine we know—'See you next Thursday morning,' it really makes people want to come back soon. Imagine: we're *expecting* them! Nobody wants to let their friends down, and that's what our regular customers are. I've got another one for you:"

> **47. Customers are strangers we want to make close friends.**

"Where else do they say, 'See you ... whenever?'" Mr. Walsh asked. "People remember us for that. It makes them feel like part of the Walsh's community, which they really are."

Candace's head was spinning with all of this new information. Mr. Walsh was on a roll, but he noticed her long enough to read her expression.

"We're almost there, Candace," he told her. "Just one more: The coffee. Let's go push carriages for a while, and then we'll jump back into this."

Pushing carriages for the customers lasted much longer than either had expected, because a rush on sale-priced pot roast brought more business than anyone had anticipated. It wasn't until the following day that teacher and student were able to take time for lessons again.

"Forty-eight?" Mr. Walsh said to Candace by way of greeting. She opened her book and read,

48. "Enjoy Your Next Coffee On Us."

"Whenever we drop the ball—in *any* way—we give our customers a free coffee as a way of saying, 'We're very sorry to let you down. That's not what you can expect from Walsh's.'"

"But I've seen associates give coffee coupons for the tiniest things!" Candace said.

"Such as?"

"Well, like that five seconds when one cashier removes her draw and a new one jumps in to take over the line."

"Nobody should have to wait for us to get our act together," Mr. Walsh said. "Not even five seconds—though that switcheroo really takes forty-four seconds."

"Forty-four seconds! Mr. Walsh, at most stores, they'll close the line entirely. Even when they don't close the line, it still takes a manager to come over to switch the computers and all that stuff. If you're unlucky enough to be in that line, you could wait five minutes or more!"

"Candace, Candace, Candace. I thought you understood by now," said Mr. Walsh, shaking his head dolefully. "We're not other stores. Closing lines, waiting five minutes, even forty-four seconds ... that's not Five-Star Customer Service! It's an insult!

"My friend, we're not competing with anyone else. We're competing with ourselves. I don't think there's one associate in this entire company who would feel proud, or even satisfied, if you told him we've done as well by our customers this year as we did last.

"Who cares what the other guys do? We don't do it that way here." Mr. Walsh unfurrowed his brow. He took a deep breath, held it, and let his tension ebb. "Sorry, but talking about bad service always makes me tense. I'll try my best to lighten up.

"So: coffee. If we're out of an item—which we rarely are, mind you—you get a free coffee for the inconvenience. Waited too long at the fish counter? Have a free coffee on us. It's particularly busy, and one of our managers noticed you walk over from an adjacent parking lot because ours was full? That's terrible! Here's a free coffee: enjoy!"

"That has got to cost you a fortune!" Candace remarked in disbelief. "How can you afford it?"

Now Mr. Walsh looked earnest. "First of all, Candace, do you have any idea of the markup on a typical cup of coffee? We can afford to give a few away; it doesn't cost us that much.

"Second, it keeps us on our game: we'd rather not give away anything, if we can help it. So, giving away a coffee reminds us that we need to improve. That reminder alone is worth the investment.

"Then there's the marketing value. Now, in our stores we've got the most delicious, professionally brewed coffee on earth—in my opinion, better than you could get in a café right there in Colombia. Mrs. Walsh is a coffee maven, and we're quite proud of what she's created here. But when you go to the grocery store, the last thing you think of is sitting down for a refreshing cup of Joe, isn't it?"

"I suppose not."

"No, it isn't. So, our little 'I'm sorry' coupons have done a great job of driving traffic to our café—where, besides coffee, you can purchase a warm sandwich, some pastry, taste a sample of whatever we're promoting that day … It's worked wonders. You see, it sure is hard to separate goodwill gestures from ploys to boost sales. This policy of mine, which started with contrition—let me assure you, I never thought it would make us money—has turned into a marketing boon."

As Candace began to ponder the last point, Mr. Walsh turned on a dime again.

"That's more than enough for today," he said. "Go back to the dorm and hang out with some friends—that's an order! No more work for you," he said kindly. "As the saying goes, All work and no play makes Candace a dull girl."

* * * * *

It was Tuesday before Candace made it back to Walsh's. But when she did, it was like she'd never left. Mr. Walsh waved when she caught his eye. He broke away from a conversation with his store manager and headed right toward her.

"Are you ready? We've got a lot to cover today," he said in his warm-but-brusque way. He caught himself. "And how was your weekend, Candace?"

Candace told him about the essay she'd had to turn in that morning for Far Eastern History class, which had occupied most of her time since their last meeting.

"I hope you got out for a beer or three Saturday night," he said.

Candace blushed, because that's exactly what she had done, but she didn't like to let on to the adults in her life that she could let her hair down when she wanted to.

"Candace," Mr. Walsh said with a wry expression. "Anybody can be good at studies, or at business, or anything else, if that's all they ever do. There's no honor in that. You've got to enjoy yourself sometimes, too. Remember, I was in college once. It was a while ago, but I'm pretty sure not too much has changed—believe it or not."

Candace didn't, but she nodded politely just the same.

"Now what's our next lesson from the Core 15?" he said.

"Well, Mr. Walsh, we've covered All-Associate Behavior, the first seven. The next seven are Process."

"Ah, yes, Process: the way things are done. What's the first one?"

> ### 49. Answer phone in two rings *or fewer.*

"I won't have my customers wait: it's as simple as that. And they deserve an actual human to pick up. And they want that person to be knowledgeable and courteous."

"Isn't that expensive? I mean, maybe a supermarket doesn't get many calls, but most businesses could never afford—"

"Wrong, Candace: company leaders can't afford *not* to treat their customers well over the phone. They're just too thick to realize it. But I'm sorry: if some companies can do it, we all can.

"Imagine if 911 made you go through one of those automated phone trees to get to an operator. 'Press one if your pants are on fire. Press two if a madman is chasing you through the house with an axe. Press three if you're having a stroke.' No, Candace, I don't think so. Walsh's customers get live humans, and they get them quickly. Even two rings are too many. Three rings? We've abused them, and they've hung up to dial Super Save."

"I was reading somewhere that some businesses have a counterpoint to that. The author said that when a company forces employees to pick up in a certain number of rings, it makes the employees rush through each call so they can get to the next one. So it actually hurts the customer experience."

"Staff sufficiently," Mr. Walsh said curtly. "Your customers deserve to have their cake and eat it too. Companies need to be smart enough to put their customers before their own lame excuses."

"Excuses are like feet," Candace said, reminding him of one of his own rules.

"They all stink out loud," Mr. Walsh agreed.

"Got it," Candace said. "One ring, maybe two. Next up? Shelves."

Mr. Walsh held up a hand. "Sorry, not now. I need you ringing on register twelve. We'll resume after the lunch rush."

* * * * *

"Alright, Francine," Mr. Walsh said to another associate, "You're on register twelve. I need Candace."

"Great!" Francine said. "That's my favorite register!"

Mr. Walsh laughed heartily. He told Candace, "Francine says that about every register. What an attitude! I wish I could clone her."

"One of me is more than enough, Bob," Francine said. "Just ask my kids."

Mr. Walsh took Candace off to pace the aisles with him. "I think our next lesson is on when to stock shelves," he said.

"Sure is," Candace said. She read,

> **50. Avoid stocking shelves while the store is open.**

"Again, this Process stuff is simple. It works like this. If we really, really need something replaced—say we're having a special on peanut butter, and there's a run on it—we'll get the stuff on the shelves while the store's open, of course. But in general we like to avoid that, because the customer finds it bothersome. Nobody likes to have to steer her cart around busy clerks with empty and half-empty boxes of stuff while they're shopping. And it looks tacky, besides. Remember, people eat—"

"—with their eyes," Candace said.

"Exactly. So we stock shelves before and after hours. What's next?"

51. Patrol the aisles

"One thing that drives people nuts when they're shopping is when they can't find a person to ask about something. Now, in a grocery store, you've got people working the outside part of the store: the deli crew, the bakers, hot foods, cheese, wine.... We've got people stationed there, so we're all set. But at most stores, there's never anybody in the center aisles.

"Here at Walsh's it's even less likely that a customer will find someone in the aisles because, as we just discussed, we don't stock shelves while the store is open. So we assign three associates in each store to patrol the aisles, just to be helpful.

"I've never really noticed—"

"You'd notice if we stopped—or, if you wander over to Johnson's, you'll notice right away that nobody's there to help you. You'll get frustrated, and you'll come back to us lickety-split! It's just one more little thing we do to spoil our customers rotten and lock them in for life."

"I can see how it would. Especially if the associates in question really know their stuff ..."

"Which they do."

"... they could offer people suggestions, like recommending the deli's fresh guacamole and perhaps some shredded Mexican cheese to complement the chips and salsa the customer is buying," Candace said.

"Absolutely!" Mr. Walsh said. "Or even, 'That national brand is good and all, but have you tried this one, Myrtle? It's a Walsh's exclusive: organic, straight from Mexico. Mrs. Walsh found it herself while on vacation down there last winter. It's even less expensive than the other brands, because it's our private label.'" Mr. Walsh said. "People love a story behind the products they buy."

Candace looked at him in wonder.

"It's another example of merchandising. We've turned the science into an art, that's all."

"So, correct me if I'm wrong, but the added payroll you put into these three associates more than pays for itself, doesn't it?"

"Once again, the question really is, How can the other guys afford *not* to do this? Payroll is only an expense if you're a knucklehead. Utilized properly, people are an investment, one that shows an immediate return. Put your people to work equipped with the right skills, and they truly are a resource, not a liability."

"Wow."

"Wow is right. Let's move this party to the produce department. I just want to watch our customers for a while. It's always nice to see the wonder on their faces as they walk into the store and see all of the beautiful colors and delectable Walsh exclusives."

* * * * *

"Next up?" Mr. Walsh said when they were safely ensconced between the bananas and the grapefruit. Candace said, "'Two to a checkout line—Max!' But I've already picked that up from your associates. It's lesson number twenty-three."

"Well, it's a big one," Mr. Walsh said. "I won't—"

"'I won't have my customers wait,'" Candace said. They shared a laugh.

"In all seriousness, Candace: if someone wants to give me her money, who am I to make her wait?! It's insane! Besides just plain rude, I am absolutely convinced that this one standard of ours brings us more business than anything else we do. You know, I've met people at parties who say, 'Oh yes, Walsh's: the store where you never have to wait in line.'"

"That is a pretty powerful tag line," Candace agreed.

"You bet it is! Do you have another SOP for me?"

"Let's see," Candace said. "Number fifty-two ..."

> **52. Carryout service (Standard. No tipping).**

114

"I say *this* is what Walsh's is best known for," Candace said. "Walsh's, where we push your carriage out to your car for you."

"And where you'll never find an empty carriage left in your parking spot. That one drives me crazy. At Walsh's, we love to spoil our customers rotten. Some don't like this pasha treatment, but most eat it up. And imagine what happens when they go to another store. They'll stand beside their carriage, waiting for the bagger to start pushing, but ... no pushing! Oh, they'll be back, alright."

"Yeah, that's my favorite signature service at Walsh's. My mom's nuts about it."

"Glad to hear it," Mr. Walsh said. "What's the next one?" He looked at his watch. "Better leave it for tomorrow. I have to visit another store right now."

"Can I tag along?" she asked.

Mr. Walsh raised an eyebrow. "Don't you have any homework to do?"

"It's Friday."

"A party to primp for?"

"Our parties go all night. I'll drop in later. Right now, I'm doing what I want to do most: I'm learning."

Mr. Walsh threw up his hands. "I surrender! Let's go."

* * * * *

In the car, they kept the conversation going. Candace read the next entry in her journal:

53. Continue the sale next week.

"This one isn't really clear to me," Candace said.

"When we have a sale," Mr. Walsh explained, "there's always someone who fails to make it to the store that week. They might be on vacation, or sick, or who knows? Or maybe, much as we hate this, we run out of the sale item—we try to err on the side of overstocking, but we still get caught by surprise sometimes.

"So now we've got someone coming to us for the sale price, and they're unhappy because they missed it. Someone else wants a rain check, which is just a big hassle all around. To spoil our customers, we always leave our sale items at the sale price one week longer than the ads say. It cures a whole host of sins."

"You do?" Candace asked, shocked.

"Every time."

"I've never heard of such a thing ..." Candace said.

Mr. Walsh laughed wickedly. "That's the point," he whispered conspiratorially. "We do what no one else has even thought to do. It's why our customers love us. It's why they keep coming back."

"I can see that," Candace said, awed by this newest revelation.

But Mr. Walsh wasn't finished. "One more Core SOP, right?" he asked.

"Well, two more, if you include the Core management practice."

"Tell ya what, then. Let's wrap it up for now. We can finish the last two later. I need you in the bakery today. How are you at decorating cakes?"

* * * * *

As it turned out, there was too much going on at the second store for Candace and Mr. Walsh to discuss her research project; it was two days before Candace and her mentor were back together. During that time, she worked around the clock, in four new departments—she even worked with the butchers in the meat department, and by the end of that stint she had gotten some experience cutting steaks herself. Not bad, she thought, though she could see why these guys were so well paid: that was hard work, and a bit bloody for her liking, as well.

Finally, Mr. Walsh found her at lunch with two associates from the cheese department. He sat down beside them.

"Good afternoon, ladies," he said. "Anything exciting happening in Cheese? Candace, I trust Martha and Anne are showing you the ropes?"

"Oh, she's a pro by now, Bob," Martha said. She was the senior associate in the Cheese department, and nobody knew cheese—or customers—like her.

"Coming from Martha, the world's foremost authority on all things cheese, that's a real feather in your cap, Candace. Good for you!"

"Stick around long enough, Candace, and you may get a trip to France like Martha," Anne said.

"Huh?" asked Candace. Martha wasn't even department manager. Mr. Walsh had sent her to France?

"I got the idea from my pals at Wegmans," piped in Mr. Walsh. "Remember I told you, if you find a great idea, make it your own. Well, Wegmans sent one of their cheese associates to Italy years ago, to tour different suppliers and get a real education on her area of expertise. They're still buzzing about it. I thought that was a terrific idea, so I sent Martha to France."

Anne piped up again. "He also sent an associate to California wine country, another to Argentina from the meat department, another to Japan to learn about Sushi from a real Sushi master—"

"Judy and I tagged along on that one," Mr. Walsh said. "The fish markets they have there are like nothing you've ever seen!"

"We have a different research trip every quarter," Anne explained.

Martha nodded. "An associate from our floral department went to Holland one year, and another went to Medallin, Colombia, just a few months ago: the City of Flowers. I think we've got every department covered with at least one associate-expert by now, haven't we, Bob?"

Mr. Walsh nodded. "You don't get to be a Walsh's Expert until you've traveled, Candace," he explained.

"A few of our Produce guys have traveled," he continued. "There's so much territory to cover. They've been to California,

Idaho, Mexico…. But I don't think anybody from dairy has traveled yet. There's too much fresh milk right around here to warrant that. Maybe someday."

"This sounds really …"

"Expensive?" Mr. Walsh finished for Candace with a fatherly wink. Turning to Martha and Anne, he said, "Candace is very concerned about how I spend our money. She thinks I'm frivolous."

Anne and Martha repeated Mr. Walsh's favorite line in unison: "Training is an investment, not an expense."

Mr. Walsh's whole face lit up. "Someone's been paying attention!"

Anne and Martha excused themselves to go back to work, leaving Mr. Walsh and Candace alone.

"Almost done with the Core 15, right?" he said.

"Two more," Candace replied. "One more from Process, and the fifteenth is just for managers." She opened her ever-present notebook and read the fourteenth Core practice.

> **54. Forgot your wallet? You can pay next time you're in.**

"I haven't seen this one in action yet," she said. "It sounds a little risky, though. Do I have it right, that if you come shopping and discover you left your money at home, you don't have to pay? You can just leave with the merchandise?" She looked uncertain. "I'm sure I have something wrong."

"Nope, not at all: you nailed it. If a customer comes shopping and finds she's left her wallet at home, we tell her to take her stuff home. No need to make a special trip back."

"No way!"

"Yes way. These are our customers. We've got to spoil them."

"But how often do they rip you off?" Candace asked, incredulous.

"Next to never. There are always people willing to take advantage, Candace. Just not as many as you'd think. We've only had a handful of problems with this since our founding.

"What we do when this situation arises is, the cashier calls over the head cashier—no need for a manager, but somebody senior has to be involved. That's just good business sense; we find our associates, especially the younger or newer ones, are our greatest theft risk—though let me assure you, employee theft is extremely rare as well."

"And you have no security cameras, I've noticed. How do you know you aren't getting ripped off even more than you think?"

Mr. Walsh laughed. "I won't spy on my customers, Candace. It's creepy. That kind of thing shows that you don't trust any of them, when the vast majority of customers are completely honest. Remember, customers are strangers you want to become—"

"Close friends," Candace finished for him.

"Exactly. And you wouldn't spy on your friends and family, would you? If you owned a store and your aunt came shopping, and she forgot her purse, wouldn't you trust her to pay later?"

"Um ... yes," Candace said weakly.

"Me, too. So, the head cashier gets the customer to sign the receipt and, if she isn't a regular, to write her address and phone number, too. Then, she's free to go."

Candace opened her mouth to protest, but Mr. Walsh held up his hand.

"It works. If it didn't, we'd change the practice."

"It's just so ... amazing," Candace said.

"I should hope so!" Mr. Walsh said. "My name's on the front of the store. It's on every bag we send home with our customers. It's on some of our food. I'm not *about* to let my company be anything less than amazing. Amazing, and really, really profitable."

"I believe that. Your stores are so much busier than any other grocer in the area ..."

"I've noticed," Mr. Walsh said with jocular smugness. Shifting gears in an instant, he said, "We'll get into the last one in the morning."

* * * * *

"The last of the Core 15 is for managers," Candace reminded Mr. Walsh the next day. She read,

> **55. Top two managers visible and engaged with customers during peak hours.**

"I've seen this one a hundred times; not just during regular peak hours, either. Your GM and assistant store manager are often in the store, and they help bag several times a day, it seems. Customers see them helping up front all day long. I think their offices must get dusted by the maintenance staff, because I never see them there—in fact, now that I think of it, I've never even noticed your managers' offices."

Mr. Walsh looked at Candace slyly. "I have a question for you. Have you ever been to *my* office?"

Candace thought hard. "You know, no. I haven't."

"Where is it?"

"Uh …" Candace racked her brain. "I suppose it's in one of the other stores. I spend most of my time here, because it's close to my dorm."

"Candace, you've never been to my office because I don't *have* an office. Not even at home."

Candace felt like a ton of bricks had just been dropped on her. "You're joking," she said.

"Not nearly. Same goes for our GMs and assistant store managers. Our department heads have paperwork to do: scheduling, ordering, and reconciling their budgets. They get a podium to work at in the back of the house, right near their department, so they can look through the window in the door and see what's going on. They stand at it. That encourages them not to linger."

"I've noticed those podiums," Candace said. "I didn't realize that's all they had."

"And we encourage them to make use of these work stations as little as possible," Mr. Walsh said. "Our top two managers in each store have less paperwork—they just have to check on the department heads' work, which means they spend some time in the conference room, meeting with the department managers. There's one computer in there, as I'm sure you've noticed, so they can review the department heads' work as necessary.

"Me? If I have any paperwork to look at, I'll do it right here, in the café. I love to be a part of things—and I don't love paperwork. My managers know that. I pay them well and train them extraordinarily well so they can do their jobs right. That makes me the most expendable man in this company. I don't have any use for an office. An office is a place to hide."

"You're expendable?"

"A leader's job is to make himself obsolete—I try to ingrain that in all of our managers, too. Our company can only grow as fast as the talent we have coming up through the ranks. A manager can't develop the talent in his department without getting out of the way and letting them do their thing."

"A leader's job is to make himself obsolete," Candace repeated, awestruck.

"By that standard, I guess I'm quite a leader. It frees me up to pioneer, to set new directions for our business. That's what a true leader's other job is. He's an inventor, a pioneer, a researcher, a dreamer, and a communicator. That last one's vital, by the way. He's got to share those dreams with his people."

"Oh," Candace said. This was a lot for her to absorb all at once.

Mr. Walsh read her expression. "We're wandering a bit far from customer service, but then, you don't get that in a vacuum. Leadership and customer service go hand in hand."

"And phone calls?" Candace asked, still hung up on this news about his nonexistent office.

"I carry my cell. My phone is always on vibrate, right here on my belt," he said, moving his jacket aside to show her. "If I get a call while I'm wandering the store, I'll walk to the back and take it—you can't do that in front of the customers, of course, because it's obnoxious to hear some guy yammering on the phone while you shop. But you see, even in the case of phone calls, I have no need for an office."

Mr. Walsh let her digest that before he continued. "We're in the people business, Candace. Our field is customer service; food is just our sub-specialty. And in a people business, you have to mix with people. You can't do that in an office.

"I stipulate that the top managers be visible and engaged during peak hours because that's when things can get hairy: despite our best efforts, that is when lines may begin to form, or we may run out of one-percent milk, or some other catastrophe."

Candace knew better than to question his use of such a strong word as catastrophe. To Mr. Walsh, any deviation from perfection was, indeed, the end of the world.

"If things are going wrong and the manager isn't visible, customers will get cranky, imagining he's hiding in his office because he doesn't care about the chaos in his store. If he's talking to his staff while his customers wait in line, those customers will know he doesn't care about them. So, our managers are engaged. They'll take off their jackets, roll up their sleeves, and bag, or jump behind the stove to prepare some hot meals, or whatever the crisis demands.

"This buys us goodwill," Mr. Walsh explained. "It's clear to the customer that, while we may have blundered by not staffing or ordering sufficiently, we do care, we are sorry, and we are getting our hands dirty, pitching in to help in a crunch."

"And you do this yourself, I've noticed."

"I'm the best-paid bagger in the business," he said with a contented look about him. "Love it; always have."

Mr. Walsh glanced at his watch. "That should do for now; it's time for me to get back to work. Mrs. Walsh wants to meet you. How about dinner at our place tomorrow night?"

"I'd love it!" Candace said.

"Terrific. Meet me here at five. I'll chauffeur you myself."

* * * * *

If Candace was nervous before her arrival at the Walsh home, Mrs. Walsh put her right at ease, greeting her with a big hug and a glass of freshly-squeezed lemonade. Their house was gorgeous inside and out, located on a quiet street in the same affluent suburb as their first store. It wasn't nearly as big or sumptuous as Candace had expected, though. It was almost ... modest.

Mrs. Walsh anticipated Candace's unspoken question. "We don't need a mansion, Candace," she said kindly. "We give most of our money to charity."

"Mrs. Walsh is as eager to feed the Third World as I am about feeding our customers," Mr. Walsh chimed in. "Call her Robin Hood: taking from comfortable Americans, giving to poverty-stricken Africans, Asians, Central and South Americans.... She's a real do-gooder."

"So are you," Mrs. Walsh said, poking her husband in the ribs in fun. "My husband, the hard-boiled business man; the closet bleeding heart."

"I'm sure Candace doesn't want to hear us squabble," said Mr. Walsh. "Let's eat!"

Mrs. Walsh served a delicious dinner, made with ingredients Candace recognized from the store: a beautiful salad, fresh halibut in a lemon-caper sauce, and for desert, pastries from the bakery. Conversation was light, centered on Candace's family and studies, and the Walsh's travels—they'd crossed the globe numerous times, and had some very unusual tales to tell.

Mr. Walsh whipped up three decaf lattes, and then launched into "shop talk" as soon as he sat back down. By now, Candace wasn't surprised in the least with his changing gears.

"Got your notebook with you, Candace?" he asked.

Mrs. Walsh formed her hands into a T. "Time out," she said. "I'm going to excuse myself. I've got the whole customer service thing memorized. I could give it to you backwards by now." Smiling kindly, she took her coffee and retreated to the library.

Mr. Walsh looked earnestly at Candace. His question was still unanswered. She pulled the notebook out of her bag with a flourish.

"Good. You won't need it," he said. "Let's see what you've learned. Fire away." With that, he sat back. It was Candace's show now.

The young pupil was flustered. "What have I learned?" she asked. "Where do I start?"

"Anywhere is fine."

"Anywhere...." She pondered that for a moment. Oh, what the heck, she thought. Best to take him at face value. She started right in.

"I've learned quite a number of things. One, to have an amazing company, you've got to have an amazing, visionary leader."

"Flattery will get you everywhere. Continue."

"Then, it is essential to employ people who really care; who want to get service right. People who share his vision."

"Now you're talking," Mr. Walsh said. He sat forward in his chair excitedly.

"Once you've got the right leadership, the right vision, and the right people, you're almost home. Right there, you've already surpassed ninety-eight percent of the companies out there."

"Yes! But Five-Star Customer Service isn't top two percent. Only the top one percent will do."

"So, you've got to teach all of these eager people how to do things right. Instituting—and upholding—standard operating procedure, such as the Core 15, is one way to make sure incredible service happens. Leading by example is without question another way."

"And …?" Mr. Walsh asked. It was clear to see that he was brimming with pride.

"And you have to talk to your associates, to carry on a continual dialogue that allows those who know (usually managers and senior associates) to share that knowledge with those who want to know (mostly newer staff members)."

"Absolutely!"

"So teaching isn't just a class once a week, or once a quarter. It isn't a five-minute 'huddle' at the start of a shift."

"Both of those are important, though!"

"Yes," Candace agreed. "And you do plenty of that stuff at Walsh's. But most of the teaching that goes on at Walsh's is done through continual two-way dialogues among workers, with managers, and even with you. All day, every day, throughout the week—"

"Throughout the day, the week, the month, and the year. Education at our company never ends; it never even takes a rest."

"Yes," Candace said. "I can see that."

"Anything else?" Mr. Walsh asked. "You haven't mentioned customers once. What about how we spoil 'em rotten?"

Candace looked at him strangely. She couldn't believe her ears.

"'What about spoiling customers?'" she repeated, dumbfounded. "What of all that *isn't* about spoiling customers?"

"So ..." Mr. Walsh said. "What you're saying is, particular practices, such as pushing carriages to our customers' cars, aren't what's important to customer service. Is that what you're telling me?"

"Of *course* that's important!" Candace exclaimed, again getting a bit flustered. "What I'm saying is that none of those *particular* behaviors matter one bit if the people doing them aren't excited to do them. If they don't live to spoil their customers. If they don't have the Customer Service Ethic. That goes for employees, managers, and the owner as well. Everybody behind the behaviors has to really be ... um ... completely behind them! Or else it isn't going to work."

Mr. Walsh looked thoughtfully at Candace for a long moment before he next spoke. "H.I.T. in action," he said.

"Hit?" Candace asked, baffled.

"H-I-T," he repeated. "H.I.T. I got it from a consultant—a husband-wife team, actually. It sums up what we do perfectly. Better open your notebook. This is your last lesson."

"Last …?" Candace was crestfallen. Mr. Walsh ignored her. She opened her notebook and wrote what he told her.

56. Employ talented consultants.

"Consultants?" Candace asked. "But you're already Five-Star! How could some outside so-called expert teach you anything about customer service, Mr. Walsh?"

"When you think you know it all, you've already started to lose the game. A fresh perspective, and even a glimmer of new information to improve yourself, is worth its weight in gold. It's how you stay ahead; after all, there's always somebody hungry on your heels, just waiting to catch you napping so he can surpass you at your own game."

"Okay, I get it. But that's not H.I.T. You were going to tell me about your big secret to getting customer service right throughout your entire organization."

"You're right. Start writing."

> **57. Make your company a H.I.T.**
> **H**ire for attitude.
> **I**nspire through pride.
> **T**rain in skills.

"That's it," Mr. Walsh said. "It's everything you'll ever need to know about running a winning organization- -and it works for everything, not just customer service. Any endeavor—business, volunteering, even the military—this is the key. Follow H.I.T., and you'll be a tremendous success.

"Now, let's go through the three parts. When you Hire—"

"No, let me!" Candace exclaimed. She caught herself. "Please," she added.

"I admire your enthusiasm. Take it away!"

Candace sat up straight in her chair. She was ready to show her stuff.

"When you Hire, select people for their attitudes, not their resumes. Sure, you need basic skills—a threshold, if you will. So for instance, the guys working on the Walsh's web site have to know web design, and you want the most skilled techies you can find for that. Your cashiers have to know some basic math, your meat department guys have to be able to cut beef into steaks before they take the job of butcher. Hiring for attitude doesn't mean you blow these threshold issues off.

"But once you've satisfied that threshold, you'll still have plenty of applicants to choose from. So, choose your new hire for her attitude. If she loves working with people, and really cares about Delighting them, then she's going to fit right in at your five-star company."

"That's right, Candace," Mr. Walsh said. "You put that well. But before we move on I have a question for you: What if you have somebody already on board who has a bad attitude? A bad apple?"

Candace looked Mr. Walsh directly in the eye. "Let 'em go."

"Isn't that a little bloodthirsty?" asked Mr. Walsh.

"We can't choose our shoe size, or our height, or the quality of our eyesight; we're stuck with what our genes hand us. But we all choose our attitudes. So if your attitude stinks? See ya. And there's no need for the boss to feel bad about it, either."

"I like it," Mr. Walsh said. "Write that one down."

58. What about the bad apples? Cut your losses.

"Good," Mr. Walsh said, looking over Candace's shoulder. "Now what about the next part of H.I.T.: Inspire. What does that mean? Conduct motivational sessions, rah-rah meetings, before work each day?"

Candace laughed. "I don't think so," she said. "I've never seen something like that at Walsh's, and I'll bet I never will. Rah-rah isn't what the Inspire part of H.I.T. is all about. After all, if you've got the right people 'on the bus,' as Jim Collins puts it, they're already completely self-motivated."

"Well said," Mr. Walsh remarked.

"Inspire through pride refers to pride in the company: bosses have to create a company that people are proud to work for. Even if you're just a maintenance guy at Walsh's, you tell people with pride, "I work at Walsh's!" You're proud of your company, and by association your job, and because of that, you're proud of yourself."

"But Candace, I take exception to one thing: you said, 'Even if you're just a maintenance guy.' There is no such thing as 'just' anything in this world. A great maintenance worker has a lot more to be proud of than a mediocre doctor, or architect, or even business owner."

Candace blushed, abashed. "You're right, of course, Mr. Walsh. And you know what? I really believe you when you say that. I think there are very few men of accomplishment such as you who honestly hold that opinion."

"Men *or women* of accomplishment, Candace," he said with a paternal wink.

She laughed. "You got me again."

"Just keeping you on your toes. Please continue. You were telling me about Inspiring through Pride. All done with that one? Can we move on to Training?"

"Almost, Mr. Walsh. One more thing I wanted to say about the second part of H.I.T. is that it goes back to the first part. Hire and Inspire create a feedback loop: when you hire the right people, they help you create an inspirational company. When your company is inspirational, attracting wonderful people is that much easier—which makes the company even more inspirational. On and on it goes."

"And that's how you stay ahead of the competition."

"Way ahead," she agreed. "The only way someone could catch Walsh's now is if you change how you do things—if you start to water down this amazing brand you've created."

It was obvious that Mr. Walsh was proud. He loved his company as if it were one of his children.

"Plenty of great brands get off track, though, Candace. You can never let up."

"Never," she agreed. "Now, about Training: if you've got the first two parts of H.I.T. right, it's a cinch to Train in skills. Enthusiastic, customer-centric associates working for a company they're intensely proud of? Those are the most willing students in the world. Academic skills have nothing to do with it—who cares what kind of an educational background they have? You give me an eager student, and I'll give you results through Training."

"That's a pretty bold claim from someone who's never taught a class before," Mr. Walsh said.

"The classroom is only a tiny part of Training, Mr. Walsh. You've told me as much a thousand times! In your supermarkets, you Train people through a constant, two-way dialogue, the mentor explaining how things are done—how you can defuse a cranky customer, for instance—and the novice asking questions, practicing, asking for and getting advice.... That's Training the Walsh's way. It's the best way there is to teach customer service skills."

"Although I *am* a big supporter of seminars. The consultants we bring in sure do help. I'm confident we wouldn't be where we are today without them."

"Yes, I'm with you," Candace laughed. "Those workshops don't happen in a vacuum, though. Your managers and associates use the stuff they learn that very same day. They add it to their SOPs."

Mr. Walsh sat back in his chair and again looked piercingly at his pupil. Candace sat there, waiting for him to speak.

Finally he said, "Candace, it sounds like you've got it. You've learned pretty much everything I have to teach you, and you've mastered that material, too—I have a feeling you won't be forgetting this stuff once you walk out my door."

Candace nodded, shifting in her seat. All this talk of being done and walking out the door concerned her terribly. She'd come to love Mr. Walsh, his company, and the many friends she'd made while researching her term paper for her consumer psychology class. She didn't want those relationships to end—especially with this remarkable man who had taught her so much.

"I've been thinking," Mr. Walsh continued. "I've been an employer for over forty years now—okay, *well* over forty years. And I like to think of myself as a fairly good judge of talent. A sharp kid like you doesn't come along very often; not that often at all.

"But as I said, I've taught you what I know. To stick around me now would only be to hold yourself back." He paused again, letting his words sink in. "What you need, if you're really going to make something out of our friendship, Candace, is access to my friends—to people like me who know customer service, and heck, business in general, and who are doing it right.

"How would you like to expand your project beyond the doors of Walsh's Supermarkets? How would you like a personal introduction to more business leaders, who can share what they know with you, the way I have?"

"How … How could I say no?!" Candace asked, mouth agape.

"Settled, then!" Mr. Walsh said, slapping his thighs and standing up so quickly that it startled Candace. "We'll get started right away. I know just the person to begin with: George Laskin, our IT solutions guru. His business is amazing! Let's give him a call!"

* * * * *

Later that night, after she had left the Walsh's home, Candace opened her notebook to add one final entry:

> **59. Always give more than you promise.**

> **60. A *lot* more!**

Be it free cooking advice in the canned food aisle, or sixty tips where you promised fifty-two, Mr. Walsh lived his life, and led his business, by this rule above all others. He did indeed spoil his customers—and his friends, like Candace—rotten!

Afterword

We hope you've enjoyed getting to know Candice, Mr. Walsh, and their friends as much as we enjoyed creating them.

What next?

The worst disservice you can do yourself is to put this book down and forget about it. We didn't write it for entertainment, although we hope it was entertaining. We wrote *Spoil 'em Rotten!* to teach our readers some of the best practices in Customer Delight—best practices that we sincerely hope you practice every day, starting today.

For much more on spoiling your customers rotten, visit us online:

www.spoilemrotten.blogspot.com

www.coineinc.com

978-0-595-42412-2
0-595-42412-0